THE
BIBLE
alive

Witness the Great Events of the Bible

Bible text John D. Clare
Original commentary Henry Wansbrough
Edited for HarperSanFrancisco/Zondervan
Brian Brown, Stan Gundry and Verlyn Verbrugge

ZondervanPublishingHouse
Grand Rapids, Michigan

HarperSanFrancisco
San Francisco, California

Divisions of HarperCollinsPublishers

Contents

THE OLD TESTAMENT

THE
BIBLE
alive

Bible Alive has been created and produced
by HarperCollins Publishers Limited
77-85 Fulham Palace Road, London W6 8JB
©HarperCollins Publishers Ltd

Project Editor Susie Elwes
Director of Photography Michael Raggett
Photography Tony May
Design Bharat Kakaiya
Production Kenneth J Clark

First published in Great Britain in 1993

Printed and bound in Italy by
ARTI GRAFICHE MOTTA

Library of Congress Cataloging-in-Publication Data

The Bible alive: be a witness to the great events
of the Bible. – 1st ed.
p.   cm.
Includes index.
Summary: Retells pivotal events in the Bible
using modern scholarship and graphic
computer techniques.
ISBN 0-06-067028-2 (alk. paper)
1. Bible stories, English. 2. Bible – History of
Biblical events – Juvenile literature. (1. Bible
stories. 2. Bible – History of Biblical events.)
BS551.2.B477 1993
220.9'505 – dc20   92-56110
                                    CIP
                                    AC

CONTENTS

THE NEW TESTAMENT

INTRODUCTION

The Bible is a record of the encounter between God and the people whom he had chosen to be his special people. It is the unfolding of this relationship. God promised their ancestor Abraham that he would make him the father of a great nation. Abraham trusted God, but it was only some 500 years later that the promise began to be fulfilled.

The encounter of God and Abraham (at first he was called Abram) begins in the fertile plain of Mesopotamia, part of the area now called Iraq. The good agricultural conditions allowed a rich civilization to develop here about 3000 BC. From there the story moves to the stony hill-country of Canaan or Palestine, a narrow strip of land between the Mediterranean Sea and the desert, where water is always in short supply, and olives and vines are the chief crop. The story also moves to Egypt, another great empire, watered by the River Nile. The pyramids had already been standing for 1500 years by the time Abraham's family were driven by hunger and thirst to take refuge in Egypt. For most of their history the Israelites (as they came to be called) were sandwiched between these two great empires, Mesopotamia and Egypt, threatened first by one powerful neighbor, then by the other. The armies of both trampled through their country, and they were powerless to resist.

The great nation promised to Abraham started from small beginnings. His descendants escaped from Egypt as slaves and – against all probability – survived a whole series of difficulties.

They wandered for forty years in the desert, where God again promised to make the people of Israel his special people.

Time after time disaster seemed inevitable. But they called on their God for help, and managed to beat off attack from stronger opponents. Their partnership with God was stormy: sometimes they neglected him, turned to other gods or refused to obey the instructions he had given them. Then their stronger neighbors oppressed them – until they remembered that he was the source of their strength, and without him they were powerless.

Twice he seemed to have deserted them completely. Once, the Ark, the sign of his protecting presence, was captured in battle. After this disaster, the Israelites demanded a king to rule them. The kings beat off their enemies and built up a strong nation. The worst disaster of all was when their capital city, Jerusalem itself, was sacked and the Israelites were dragged into exile in Babylon. For a time this seemed to be the end of them as a nation, and the end of their relationship with God. After a time, however, they reflected on their situation, and saw that this too was part of their learning process. Their relationship with God needed to change and become less national. The exile in Babylon also scattered the Jews throughout the world; from Babylon they spread all over the Mediterranean world, and their descendants have continued to spread still further. After less than a hundred years, a new ruler allowed the exiles in Babylon to return to Jerusalem and re-found their state. The return to and the rebuilding of Jerusalem brings to an end this era of Jewish history.

After returning to Jerusalem, the great empires of Persia, Macedon, Syria and Rome in turn dominated the ancient Near East; the Jews were for the most part an oppressed people. They longed to be free. They hoped more and more intensely for a leader who would make the kingship of their God a reality.

Christians believe that this leader was Jesus Christ. His story and that of his followers are told in the New Testament and the second half of this book.

The Bible

The Bible is a book which comprises a small library of books. Some of the books contain history, others laws. Some were written in poetry, others in prose. Some of the books contain prayers used by God's people. Others record warnings and encouragement spoken to them by their holy men in God's name.

What made this people special was that God had chosen them as his own people. The Bible describes the origin and development of their encounter with him.

The narratives of their ancestors were very important to the Israelites, since it was to them that the promises had been given. They passed these stories on orally to their children and their children's children very carefully. At some point they were written down by the inspired writers of Scripture. Recent discoveries of other ancient documents by archaeologists have shown just how accurate these accounts in the Bible are.

The interest of the writers was not just straight-forward history. Rather, they wanted to tell the religious implications of their history – the story behind the story. They wrote about God and his attitude to his people, and the people and their attitude to God

This God was the Lord of the world and its history, sharing his rights with no other, controlling all nations as he willed. It was not possible to make any image or picture of him, not possible to control or even to imagine him. He was an awesome as well as loving God.

Above
*A large
Philistine jar.*

Below
*Sheep grazing on the
Judaean hills.*

In the beginning God created heaven and earth. Earth was an empty and formless chaos, and the spirit of God hovered over the deep waters. Then God said, "Let there be light", and there was light. God saw that the light was good. He separated light from darkness. God called the light "day", and he called the darkness "night". And there was evening and morning – the first day.

On the following days, God created the sea and the dome of the sky, dry land and plants, the sun and moon, and living creatures – fishes and great reptiles from the sea, and birds in the air. Finally, on the sixth day, God made the animals, and human beings.

God looked at everything he had made, and saw that it was very good. And there was evening and morning, a sixth day.

On the seventh day, God rested from all the work he had done. So God blessed the seventh day and set it apart as a special day. That is how the universe was created.

from Genesis, chapter 1, verse 1 to chapter 2, verse 4

Another account
Before the Lord made the earth and the heavens, there were no plants and no seeds. The Lord had not yet made it rain, and there were no human beings to cultivate the earth. In that day, the Lord shaped man out of the clay of the ground. He breathed the breath of life into his nostrils, and man became a living being.

The Lord made the man fall into a deep sleep. While he slept, he took one of his ribs and made woman out of the rib.

from Genesis, chapter 2, verses 4–7, 21–22 to chapter 2, verse 4

Right
The earth became fertile.

God separated light from darkness.

"In the beginning God"
The Hebrew Scriptures always assume and never argue for God's existence. Although everything else had a beginning God has always been.

Genesis 1.1 to 2.3 is a general account of creation that emphasizes that everything that is owes its existence to God and because of that it is good, indeed very good. God gave human beings the responsibility to care for his creation rather than exploiting, wasting or despoiling it. Beginning with Genesis 2.4 we have a second account of creation, which focuses on the beginning of human history.

A new name for God is introduced here, the personal and covenant name of God that emphasizes his personal relationship with his people. In the original Hebrew in which the Old Testament is written, although vowels were spoken, no vowels were used in the written form. The letters Y H W H were written as the name of God, but because that name was too sacred to pronounce we do not know, even today, what the full word is. Sometimes it is written as Yahweh; sometimes Jehovah. Because the Jews used as a replacement the word meaning Lord, out of respect, most English translations have represented this as Lord. We shall follow this convention in the book.

Later the Scriptures tell how God told Moses his name, as a sign of special friendship. Its meaning is uncertain, but it is probably connected with the verb "to be". It may mean "the one who gives existence" or "the one who is". So it expresses the belief that all existence comes from God.

THE GARDEN OF EDEN

The Lord planted a garden in Eden, in the East, and there he put the man he had shaped. He made trees grow there that were beautiful and good for food. In the middle of the garden he planted the Tree of Life and the Tree of Knowledge. The Lord gave the man just one commandment: "You can eat from any of the trees in the garden except the Tree of Knowledge. You shall not eat from that tree; the moment you eat from it you are doomed to die."

Above
In the beginning God created the earth.

Now the snake was the most cunning of all the animals the Lord had made. It said to the woman, "You won't die if you eat from the tree in the middle of the garden. God knows that the moment you eat from it your eyes will be opened and you will be like gods, able to tell what things are really like." So she took some of the fruit and ate it; then she gave some to her husband, and he ate it too. Their eyes were opened, and they realized they were naked. So they sewed fig-leaves together and made loincloths for themselves.

They hid, but the Lord found them. Adam blamed Eve, and Eve blamed the snake. The Lord condemned the snake to crawl on its stomach and expelled Adam and Eve from Eden. He condemned the woman to experience pain in childbirth. Finally he condemned the man to labor all the days of his life to make a living.

from Genesis, chapter 2, verse 8 to chapter 3, verse 19

The origin of evil

God placed Adam and Eve in a place and a state of perfect happiness and innocence called the Garden of Eden. In Hebrew, "Eden" means "pleasure," "Adam" means simply "man," he stands for all people. "Eve" is explained as "mother of the living." They only need accept that everything is a gift from the Lord and obey his one commandment not to eat from the Tree of Knowledge and so usurp God's position.

The account in Genesis describes the origin of sin and the fall of humankind. Sin is the state of separation of humanity from God caused by rebellion, putting ourselves where God should be. The sin of Adam and Eve is described in terms typical of every human sin. The temptation is to be too clever, to try to outwit God and seek a knowledge which is forbidden.

The story of the fall also reflects a common reaction to failure: trying to put the blame on someone else, then the feeling of shame and trying to hide, first their nakedness and then from God. Man and woman are shut out of the Garden of Eden, but with a promise that the snake, the Evil One, will eventually be conquered.

The Lord told the snake: "I will put hatred between your offspring and the woman's offspring – he shall bruise your head, but you shall bruise his heel."

A river flowed out of Eden to water the garden where man and woman went naked and were not ashamed.

Above
The snake, condemned to crawl on its stomach.

CAIN AND ABEL

Adam and his wife Eve had two sons. The first she called Cain, saying, "I have produced a son." Then she gave birth to Abel, his brother. Abel was a shepherd, but Cain was a farmer. In time, Cain made an offering to the Lord from his crops. At the same time, Abel sacrificed the first-born lamb from his flock, and gave the best parts of it as an offering.

The Lord preferred Abel's offering to Cain's. Cain resented this, and he scowled. The Lord asked, "Why are you resentful and sullen? If you are good, you will be able to hold your head up. If not, sin is crouching at the door; he wants you, but you can overcome him." Cain, however, said to Abel, "Let us go out into the field," and when they got there, he attacked and killed him.

"Where is your brother?" The Lord asked Cain. He replied, "How should I know? Is it my job to take care of my brother?" Then the Lord said, "What have you done? Your brother's blood is crying out to me from the soil! You are cursed, and you shall be a fugitive and a wanderer on the earth."

Cain said to the Lord, "Such punishment is too heavy to bear! If I am an outlaw and a nomad, anyone who meets me will kill me." So the Lord put a protective mark on Cain, so that no one who met him would kill him. Then Cain left the Lord's presence, and lived in the land of Nod, east of Eden.

from Genesis, chapter 4, verses 1–16

Adam and Eve's children
Because of the fall, unlike their parents, Cain and Abel did not live in a state of perfect happiness and innocence.

This is a story of human rivalry between brothers, about temptation and failure. However, just like the story of Adam and Eve, it does not end in despair. The Bible demonstrates that God still loved even the murderer and put on him a special mark of protection.

Cain appears again later in the Bible as the ancestor of all metalworkers. The first metal used was bronze, which is an alloy of copper and tin. It came into use about 3000 BC, and the first metalworkers in Palestine were skilled craftsmen, wandering (like Cain) from place to place.

Hebrew names
Names were very significant to the Hebrews. They felt if you named something, you gave it existence or shaped its existence. Most personal names have a meaning. The Hebrew for "I have produced" is *caniti*, which has the same basic sound as *Cain*.

The name of God
Hebrews also believed that to know someone's name gave power over that person. When the Lord revealed himself to Moses in the burning bush Moses demanded that the Lord tell him what his name was.

The Lord replied: "Tell the people I am Who I am (Or I am what *I shall reveal myself* to be)". Human beings can never have power over the Lord. We only know him as he reveals himself to us.

13

The Lord saw that people were wicked, with evil thoughts in their hearts. He was sorry that he had made them. So the Lord said, "I will blot out people from the face of the earth." One man, however, was different from the others – Noah. The Lord thought well of him.

God said to Noah, "I have decided to destroy all people, because the world is full of their wickedness. Make an ark of good wood. Make it 300 cubits long, 50 cubits wide and 30 cubits high. In a week's time I am going to send torrential rain."

True enough, seven days later, down came the floods of rain. It rained for forty days and forty nights. Noah took animals into the ark with him. He took a male and a female of every species, and the Lord shut him in. The waters covered the mountains. Every living thing died.

After ten months the waters went down. Twice Noah sent out a dove to see if there was any dry land. The third time, the dove did not return. God said to Noah, "Leave the ark, you, your family and the animals."

Then Noah built an altar to the Lord. He offered sacrifices on the altar. When the Lord noticed the soothing smell, he said, "I will never destroy every living thing again."

Then God said to Noah, "I am making my contract with you, that a flood shall never again destroy all living things. As the sign of this I set my rainbow in the sky."

from Genesis, chapters 6–9

The evidence

Archaeologists have dug through thick layers of silt, washed down from the upper Tigris and Euphrates, giving evidence of a great flood thousands of years ago.

The excavation of Nineveh in the mid-nineteenth century uncovered a large number of clay tablets. After deciphering the writing some of them proved to be an account of the flood from the standpoint of Babylonian gods.

In many ways the account is similar to the biblical record of the flood and is a definite indication that there must have been a massive flood, if not over the entire earth, at least over the inhabited world. In the biblical account this flood came as a result of God's reaction to increasing human sin. His purpose was to cleanse the world of sin.

Only one man, Noah and his family, found favor in the eyes of God and were spared.

The ark

A cubit is the length of a forearm, from elbow to fingertips, just under half a metre. (That was the longest Hebrew measure. All the Hebrew measures were based on hand and arm: 24 finger-joints = 6 palm-breadths = 2 finger-spans = 1 cubit.) So the ark was to be 150 metres long by 25 metres wide.

There have been numerous unconfirmed reports of sightings of the remains of the ark in the region of Mount Ararat. Contemporary politics in that volatile region of our world has made it impossible for large-scale scientific expeditions to ascertain the legitimacy of these claims.

THE TOWER OF BABEL

At one time everybody spoke the same language and used the same words. As people migrated from the East, they settled on the plain of Babylon. They used bricks for stone and tar for mortar. They said to one another, "Come on, let's build a city, with a huge tower reaching to the heavens."

The Lord went down to see the city and tower the men were building. He said, "They are united and speak the same language. This is just the start. Soon they will be able to do anything. Come on, let's go down and turn their language into babbling, so they won't understand one another."

So the Lord went down and scattered them all over the world. They stopped building the city. That is why the place was called Babel, because there the Lord made a babble of the languages of earth.

from Genesis, chapter 11, verses 1–9

Overleaf
The people began to build a tower in their city.

Ziggurats

On the plains of Mesopotamia several ziggurats are still to be seen. These are huge stepped towers, built 5000 years ago of mud-brick. The base is square, and then they rise in three (or even five) layers, each some twenty metres high, and each layer some twenty metres in from the last. There is a monumental flight of steps, leading from one layer to the next. The effect is rather like a square three-tiered wedding cake, with a staircase up it. They were used in sacred rites, and probably had a small temple on top. One of the first such ziggurats to be discovered was at Borsippa. This tower has been split right down the middle by lightning, and so was long considered to be the Tower of Babel itself.

The origin of languages

It is surprising that different people speak different languages. Why do they not all speak the same? The differences in language are often the cause of misunderstanding and enmity. Here these differences are explained as a punishment for sin. The sin of these people was to try unitedly to reach heaven by their own power – rather like the sin of Adam and Eve when they tried to gain forbidden knowledge by their own efforts. So the peoples were split up into different language-groups to prevent them attempting such a sin again. At the same time this is a condemnation of the pagan worship of Mesopotamia, and especially a pun on the name Babylon ("*babilu*" in the original, and in Hebrew *balel* means "to confuse").

The language of the Scriptures

Several closely related languages were spoken in biblical lands, as similar to each other as French is to English. Most of the Jewish Scriptures were written in Hebrew, but some are in Aramaic. Both scripts are read from right to left and only consonants, not vowels, are written.

What lies ahead

The first eleven chapters of Genesis describe what can be called universal history, that is, the creation of the world and especially of the human race, and the persistent failure of humankind to acknowledge God as the supreme Lord and to obey him.

The story of Abraham, which comes next in the Bible, is of a different kind. It focuses on the history of one particular man and the nation which descended from him.

Below
A clay figure found in Mesopotamia, made about 4000 years ago.

Above
Baked clay chariot found in Syria, made 3000 years ago. Originally the model included shaft and draught animals.

ABRAM LEAVES HARAN

Terah took his son Abram, his grandson Lot and Abram's wife Sarai. Together they left Ur of the Chaldeans to go to the land of Canaan. Having reached Haran, however, they settled there, and there Terah died.

The Lord said to Abram, "Leave behind your country, family and home and go to a land that I will show you. I will make you the founder of a great nation."

Abram left Haran when he was seventy five years old. He took Sarai his wife, Lot his brother's son, all the possessions they had gained in Haran and all the slaves they had acquired, and set out for the land of Canaan. Abram went through Canaan to the sacred place at Shechem, by the oak of Moreh. The Lord appeared to Abram and said, "I will give this land to your descendants." So he built an altar there to the Lord. From there he moved to the mountain east of Bethel, and there he built another altar to the Lord.

from Genesis, chapter 11, verse 31 to chapter 12, verse 8

Two stages

The Scriptures record Abram's move to Canaan in two stages. In the first stage he went with his father Terah from Ur of the Chaldees to Haran where they settled. Then suddenly without any warning, God summoned Abram to leave Haran, this comfortable existence among rich city-traders, and move to the stony land of Palestine, or Canaan as it was then called.

All God offered was the promise that Abram was to be the founder of a great nation. Abram knew nothing about this God – till then he had lived among people who worshipped the moon – but he gave up all his security for this one promise. It was a great act of trust, for he was getting old and had no child to start off the promised great nation!

The places on Abram's route show that he was a nomad shepherd. He kept away from the big towns of Canaan, lived in tents and pastured his flocks of sheep and herds of goats on the edge of civilization. Such nomads still exist in Palestine today.

Ur of the Chaldeans

The city of Ur lies on the flat plains near the mouth of the River Euphrates, and was the center of a great kingdom, 2700–2000 BC.

The remarkable number of gold ornaments and jade statues found in the tombs there shows that it was a rich centre of trade. There are women's head-dresses with delicate leaf-work in gold, and chariots with gilded shafts. A gigantic ziggurat still dominates the ruins. The chief gods worshipped were the sun and the moon, as often under the clear skies of Mesopotamia.

From there Abram's father took him and his family to Haran, another rich centre of trade – also a city where the moon was worshipped.

Schechem

Shechem had been an important city in Canaan already for over 1000 years. It lies on the only road crossing Palestine through the mountains from East to West. It has a pleasant spring of water. Abram would have come here after fording the River Jordan. It was one of the garrison towns of the Egyptians who ruled the land. In later times it became one of the important centers of Israelite worship. The biblical writer shows why the Lord here renewed his promise to Abram, and why Abram claimed the place for the Lord by building an altar there.

*Above
A model of a wagon drawn by bulls. It was made in copper about 2000 BC.*

Abram led his people and their flocks out of Haran.

MELCHIZEDEK

Right
Abram and his men.

Five rulers from the region of the Dead Sea were defeated by a rival alliance of four eastern kings. Abram's nephew Lot was among those captured in the city of Sodom.

One man escaped, however, and reported this to Abram the Hebrew, who was camping by the oak trees of Mamre the Amorite. When Abram learned that his kinsman had been captured, he called together all his followers and followed the four kings to Dan. Dividing his men into groups, he defeated the enemy in a surprise night attack and chased them as far as

Hobnah, north of Damascus. He captured all the loot and prisoners they had taken, and rescued his nephew Lot.

Then Abram returned from his victory over the kings. Melchizedek, who was king of Salem and priest of God Most High, took bread and wine to Abram. He blessed him and said,

"God Most High, who made heaven and earth, bless Abram! God Most High, who gave victory over the enemy, be praised!"

Abram gave Melchizedek a tenth of all the loot he had captured.

from Genesis, chapter 14, verses 1–20

Abram defeated the alliance of kings. Melchizedek brought out bread and wine to greet him.

The fight for land

We need to know more than the story given in the Bible tells us to understand exactly what was happening at the time. Abram and his little group of 318 retainers took on a great international alliance of kings in order to rescue Abram's nephew, Lot. Both Abram and Lot had prospered so much by this time that their flocks were too large to pasture in one place. So they had agreed to separate; Lot moved into the richer Jordan plain, while Abram stayed in the stony hills. Abram was left in peace by the marauding kings, while Lot's rich territory was plundered.

Abram the Hebrew

Abram is here called a "Hebrew" for the first time. In the Bible this term always refers to Abram and those descended from him; it is an ethnic term.

Melchizedek

Melchizedek is here called king of Salem (Salem means "peace"), probably a shortened form of "Jerusalem". This is the first mention in the Bible of the great city. It was an ancient, independent fortress-city, which the Israelites could not conquer till the time of David, nearly 1000 years later. The king, Melchizedek, was also a priest. He recognized Abram as his equal by exchanging gifts with him and prayed that God Most High might bless Abram. Abram recognized Melchizedek's sacred position by offering him a tenth of all the booty.

Christians have seen Melchizedek as a foreshadowing of Jesus. Jesus is called "a priest of the line of Melchizedek" to distinguish his priesthood from that of the Israelite Temple-priests. His sacrifice was also in the Holy City of Jerusalem. The bread and wine offered by Melchizedek have been seen as symbols of the bread and wine used at Jesus' Last Supper.

Below
King Melchizedek.

Abram said, "O Lord God, I am still childless, and my heir is my slave, Eliezer of Damascus." The Lord said to him, "Your own son shall be your heir, and you will have as many descendants as there are stars in the heavens. I am the Lord, who brought you out from Ur of the Chaldeans, to give you this land to possess."

Abram said, "O Lord God, how can I be sure that I will possess this land?" the Lord told him, "Bring me a heifer three years old, a she-goat three years old, a ram three years old, a turtledove and a young pigeon." So Abram brought them, split them all in two (except the birds), and laid out the halves opposite each other. A deep sleep came over Abram. When it was dark, a smoking fire-pot and a flaming torch passed between the pieces.

Abram's name was changed to "Abraham" (meaning "father of nations"), and Sarai's to "Sarah" (meaning princess).

One day the Lord appeared to Abraham as he sat by the door of his tent. Suddenly, in front of him were three men. He bowed to the earth and said, "Lord, please honor me with a visit."

The men asked, "Where is Sarah?"

"She is in the tent," replied Abraham. The Lord said, "I promise that I will return in the spring and Sarah shall give birth to a son." Now Sarah was listening at the tent-door. She laughed to herself, for both she and Abraham were far too old to have children.

from Genesis, chapters 15–18

Below
Grain is ground to flour in a stone quern.

The contract
God had promised to make Abraham the father of a great nation. Abraham and his wife Sarah, however, were growing older and older without having any child, and they began to despair of having a child as their heir. So God renewed his promise in the form of a solemn contract.

Contracts from the same date and area have been discovered, which explain how they were drawn up. The people making the contract slaughter animals and cut them in half, making a path between the halves. Then they walk between the halves of the animals as a sign that they are also willing to be cut in half if they break their oath. In this case, however, God alone passed between the halves of the victims. His presence was symbolized by the fire which Abraham saw in his dream. In this contract only God binds himself by oath. Abraham did not pass between the victims because he did not promise to do anything. He had only to trust in God and receive God's promise.

In confirmation of the promise their names were changed. As Abraham means "father of nations", so Sarah's name "princess" suggests that she will be a mother of kings.

The promise
To welcome guests is a basic law of nomads. Abraham welcomed these three travellers with traditional courtesy before he realized that they were God's representatives. In return he was promised a son within a year. Sarah's laugh is a clever pun on the name of her future son, for "laughs" in Hebrew is almost exactly *isaac*. The pun will occur several times in the story of Isaac.

Above
Flocks of sheep.

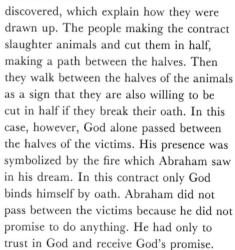

Abram saw thr[e]e strangers approach[ing] his tent.

SODOM AND GOMORRAH

The Lord told Abraham, "I have heard many complaints about Sodom and Gomorrah. They seem terribly wicked places. I will go down to see if it is as bad as I am told." Abraham, however, argued with the Lord, saying, "Are you sure you want to destroy the good people along with the wicked people? The judge of the whole world should act with justice."

That evening the Lord's two messengers went to Sodom. Abraham's nephew Lot was sitting at the gate, and he persuaded them to stay the night at his house. Before bedtime a great crowd surrounded Lot's house and demanded that he hand over the two strangers. Lot went out and tried to stop them, but they ignored him. "Out of our way, foreigner!" they said and they tried to force their way in. The Lord's messengers, however, pulled Lot back into the house and struck the crowd with blindness.

When morning came, the two messengers took Lot and his wife by the hand and led them out of the city, because the Lord had mercy on him. They said, "Flee for your life. Don't look back or stop. Flee to the hills, or you will be destroyed." Time after time, Lot delayed and argued. Finally he persuaded them to let him go instead to the small nearby town of Zoar. They promised not to destroy it.

Then the Lord rained fire and brimstone on Sodom and Gomorrah, and destroyed them, along with all the cities of the valley, their inhabitants and their crops. Lot and his family were saved, except for Lot's wife, who looked back, and was turned into a pillar of salt.

from Genesis, chapter 18, verse 20 to chapter 19, verse 26

Above
Lot, his wife and his two daughters fled the city before it was destroyed.

The people of Sodom surrounded Lot's house and demanded that he should bring out the strangers who were staying with him.

The sin of Sodom
For a nomad people like the Hebrews the worst kind of sin was to refuse hospitality to strangers, or to abuse them. Thus the desire on the part of the residents of Sodom to mistreat the two visitors of Lot demonstrated how intense their sin was in the eyes of the Lord. In reaction to this sin the Lord destroyed the cities.

Abraham the Lord's friend
Abraham speaks to "the judge of the whole world" in a frank and open way, as someone talking to a friend. This is one of many examples in Genesis that indicate the cordial and friendly relationship between Abraham and God. Later Scriptures apply to Abraham the title "God's friend." To this day the Muslims call Abraham "El Khalil, the Beloved Friend of God."

The cities
The cities of Sodom and Gomorrah have traditionally been said to have existed at the southern end of the Dead Sea. This expanse of water, about 80 kilometres by 16, is 400 metres below the level of the Mediterranean Sea. Water flows into it from several rivers, but no water flows out; it just evaporates in the intense heat, forming salt and sulphur deposits. Around it lies a dead moon-landscape: an eerie stillness and a sulphurous smell. Every now and then there is a strange pillar of eroded rock.

When the water skin was empty Hagar left her son Ishmael to die.

Sarah sent her maid Hagar to sleep with Abraham and Hagar gave him a son named Ishmael. Later, however, Sarah gave birth to Isaac; "Everyone who hears about this will laugh at me," she said. At eight days old, Isaac was circumcised by Abraham.

Isaac grew up. On the day he was weaned on to solid food, Abraham held a great feast. Sarah, however, saw Ishmael making fun of her son Isaac. So she said to Abraham, "Drive out this slave-woman and her son; a slave-woman's son will not share the inheritance with my son Isaac." Abraham was very distressed for his son Ishmael.

Nevertheless, early next morning, Abraham got up and gave Hagar some bread and a skin of water and sent her away. She left, carrying the child on her back, and wandered aimlessly in the desert around Beersheba. When the water in the skin was used up, she abandoned the child under a bush, and went to sit down a short distance away. "I can't bear to watch the child die," she said.

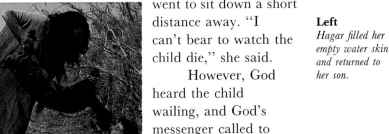

However, God heard the child wailing, and God's messenger called to Hagar, "What's the matter, Hagar? Don't be afraid. God has heard the boy crying. Help the boy up. Take him by the hand. I will make his descendants into a great nation." Then God opened her eyes, and she saw a well of water. She filled the skin with water, and gave the boy a drink. God was with the boy as he grew. He lived in the desert of Paran, and became an expert archer.

from Genesis, chapter 21, verses 1–21

Left
Hagar filled her empty water skin and returned to her son.

Hagar's child

In the nomad society of the desert an heir was all-important. Unless there were young people to take over, no one would support the aging generation. So the laws allowed a wife who had no children to give one of her slave-women the task of bearing a child with her husband on her own behalf. There were strict regulations preventing the slave-girl becoming too powerful. If she did, the wife could demand that she be sent away.

This is what happened with Abraham and Sarah. Sarah seemed unable to produce a child. So she gave her slave-woman, Hagar, to Abraham, to be the mother of a child by him in her place. Then came the visit of God's messengers, and Sarah produced her own child for Abraham, Isaac. (Note two more puns on Isaac's name – *isaac* means almost exactly "laughs" or "makes fun of".) Hagar broke the regulations, and Sarah demanded that Hagar and Ishmael be sent away, so legally Abraham had to agree.

Ishmael the archer

To the south of the hill-country where Abraham pastured his flocks lies the great desert of the Negeb (*negeb* means "dry" in Hebrew).

This story explains both what happened to Hagar and her child, and the origin of the Ishmaelites. The Ishmaelites were Arabian tribes who later lived in this area and made their living by trading in slaves and other merchandise. There was fierce hostility between the two peoples who claimed descent from these two sons of Abraham.

ABRAHAM IS TESTED AND ISAAC IS SAVED

God tested Abraham's faith. "Take your son – your only son, Isaac, whom you love so much – and go to the country of Moriah. I will show you a high place, and there you must sacrifice him as a burnt offering."

Next morning, Abraham got up early, cut the wood for the burnt offering, put a saddle on his donkey and set off to go to Moriah. He took with him two young men of his household, and Isaac. On the third day Abraham spotted the place in the distance. "Stay here with the donkey," he told the young men. "The lad and I are going over there to worship God; we'll be back soon."

Abraham gave Isaac the wood to carry, while he took the knife and the fire, and they walked along together.

"Father!" said Isaac to Abraham.

"I am here," replied Abraham.

"I see the fire and the wood, but where is the lamb for the sacrifice?" Isaac said.

"God will give us a lamb to sacrifice," Abraham reassured him.

When they came to the high place, Abraham built an altar and set out the wood properly upon it. He tied up Isaac and put him on the altar. Then he took the knife and raised it ready to kill his son. At that moment God's messenger called to him from heaven, "Don't kill or harm the lad; I know now that you really trust God, because you were prepared to give me your only son." Abraham looked up. He saw a ram caught by its horns in a bush, and he sacrificed the ram instead.

from Genesis, chapter 22, verses 1–13

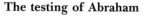

Abraham built an altar and set out the wood on it.

The testing of Abraham

This command to sacrifice his son was the climax of all the tests of Abraham's trust in God. Isaac was Abraham's only hope in his old age, the only possibility of any future for Abraham and his family. So Abraham was willing to entrust his whole self to God in blind obedience, until God showed him that his trust was rewarded.

Mount Moriah

According to the writer of Chronicles, Mount Moriah, where the sacrifice took place, was the mountain on which the Temple of Solomon came to be built in Jerusalem. The actual spot was identified as the Holy of Holies, the very center of the Temple, where only the high priest himself was allowed to enter once a year to sacrifice. The same stark, bare rock now forms the center of the Dome of the Rock, an Islamic mosque built on the site of the Temple. The rock can still be seen.

Child sacrifice

Several of the ancient peoples around Israel practised child sacrifice. It happened even in Israel in time of crisis, in spite of being strictly forbidden; it was called "sacrifice to Molech". The sacrifice of one's child is a final demonstration of a willingness to go to any lengths to turn away a threat of destruction. The Israelites believed all life came from God and was a special gift to each individual from God. In Israel the first-born of any domestic animal must be sacrificed to God or be paid for by a ritual sacrifice. So the first son to be born to a human couple was sacred to God and was considered to belong to God until he had been "bought back" by a ritual sacrifice or a payment of five shekels of silver.

Right
A simple fire was kept burning at all times. Travellers carried smouldering embers with which to light a fire.

Below
Bronze daggers were decorated and often inscribed with their owner's name.

Overleaf
Rebekah left her family and went to Canaan to be married to Isaac.

When he became very old indeed, Abraham summoned his servant Eliezer, and said, "Go to my homeland, to my relatives, to find a wife for my son Isaac."

Eliezer swore a most solemn oath to do this. Then he took ten camels and went to the city in Mesopotamia where Abraham's brother Nahor lived. When he arrived at the well outside the city walls, he made his camels kneel down. It was evening – the time when the women of the city went to the well to draw water. Eliezer prayed, "O the Lord, God of my master Abraham, let me succeed today. If I say to one of the girls, 'May I have a drink from your water-jar?' please let her reply, 'Have a drink, while I water your camels too.' Then I shall know that she is the right one."

Everything happened as Eliezer had asked. Even before he had finished his prayer, Nahor's granddaughter Rebekah came out, carrying a water-jar on her shoulder. She was beautiful, and not only gave Eliezer a drink, but watered his camels as well! Eliezer gave her a gold nose-ring, and two huge gold bracelets for her arms. Rebekah took him to her home, but he refused to accept the family's hospitality until he had told them about his mission. Then he asked Rebekah's brother, Laban, whether he would agree to Rebekah marrying Isaac. Laban gave his consent and Rebekah agreed to leave immediately.

Isaac had moved his camp from the "Well of the One Who Sees", and was in the Negeb. One evening, as he was wandering in the fields, he looked up and saw camels coming towards him. When she saw him, Rebekah got down from her camel and covered her face with her veil. Isaac took her to his tent, and she became his wife, and he loved her.

from Genesis, chapter 24

Below
Rebekah chosen as a wife for Isaac.

Eliezer's oath

Eliezer swore a specially solemn oath, since he was swearing by Abraham's hope of future generations. Abraham was determined to find a wife for his son within his own clan to avoid a marriage with the people of the land in which he was living. Abraham was on his death-bed. In his turn, Isaac's son Jacob too will return to his own clan to find a wife.

Settling down in Canaan

When Abraham's wife Sarah died, Abraham bought a field as a burial-plot for her and the family. A burial-plot is the first sign of nomads becoming settled. It becomes a permanent base for a wandering family. They carry the dead round with them until they return to the burial-plot. For Abraham and his descendants, the burial-plot which they purchased served as a down payment that eventually the Lord their God would give them the entire land of Canaan.

Isaac

Isaac is a vaguer figure in the Bible than his father Abraham or his son Jacob. The stories about him concern disputes between his herdsmen. The place-names show that he moved around the northern edge of the Negeb desert, not far from Abraham's burial-plot at Hebron.

Above
A delicate silver brooch in the form of lions above two necklaces made of gold, grainelian, lapis lazuli and rock crystal. Below the necklaces are two gold buttons.

ISAAC BLESSES JACOB

Isaac grew old and became blind. He called for Esau, his elder son (who had red hair), and said, "I am going to die soon. Take your bow and arrows, go out into the fields and kill a deer for me. Cook it and give it to me to eat. I want to give you my blessing before I die."

Rebekah, however, overheard Isaac talking to Esau. While Esau was away hunting she said to Jacob, "Take two fat young goats from the flock and I'll cook them. You can take the food into your father, and he'll give you his blessing."

Jacob hesitated: "Esau is hairy all over, and my skin is smooth. If my father touches me, he'll know I am playing a trick on him, and I'll get a curse, not a blessing." Rebekah answered, "Then let the curse fall upon me, my son." She gave Esau's best clothes to Jacob to wear, and then put the skins of the goats on his arms and neck. Jacob went to his father. "Which of my sons is this?" asked Isaac. "Your elder son, Esau," Jacob replied. "I have done as you told me."

So Isaac blessed him: "May God give you the dew from heaven and the riches of the fields. May peoples serve you, lord of your brothers."

Soon after, Esau came in. "Who are you?" asked Isaac. "Your elder son," Esau answered. "Who, then, brought the food I have just eaten? I gave him my last blessing! It is too late to take it back." When Esau realized what had happened, he shouted bitterly, "Give me your blessing too, Father!" Isaac replied, "Your brother deceived me. He has stolen your blessing for ever."

from Genesis, chapter 27, verses 1–35

Isaac tricked

This is an account of deliberate cunning and careful deception. It shows the Hebrews' belief in the power of God's blessing and their single-minded striving for this blessing. According to customs of that day, solemn words spoken on an oath before one's god could never be retracted. Thus, once Isaac had given his blessing to his younger son he could not cancel or withdraw it: God's word had been spoken.

Two rival nations

The result of the rivalry of these two brothers is the rivalry of two nations. Jacob was the ancestor of Israel. Although he was the younger brother, he received the promise of God to be father of a great nation. For hundreds of years, however, there was rivalry between Israel and their southern neighbors, the tribes of Edom, in the hills of Seir. The Edomites were rough hunters, unlike the Israelites, who were herdsmen. *Edom* in Hebrew means "red," and *seir* means "hairy." Esau is both of these.

Names also play a part in another story of Jacob supplanting Esau (*jacob* means "supplant"). Esau came in one day from hunting, famished, and asked his brother for some *red* stew Jacob was cooking. Jacob refused until Esau promised to hand over his rights and privileges as the elder brother, in payment for the plate of stew.

Jacob fled from his brother Esau, and went to Mesopotamia to live with his uncle Laban.

After a month, Laban said to Jacob, "It isn't right that you should work for me for nothing, just because you are a relative. What shall your wages be?" Now Laban had two daughters, Leah (the elder), and Rachel (the younger). Leah had lovely eyes, but Rachel was shapely and beautiful. Jacob had fallen in love with Rachel, so he said, "I will work seven years for you, if you will let me marry Rachel." Laban answered, "Rather you have my daughter than anyone else! Stay here with us!" So Jacob worked seven years for Rachel, and the time seemed like only a few days, because he loved her.

Finally, Jacob said to Laban, "I have served my time. Let me marry my wife." So Laban sent invitations to all the men of the village, and held a wedding-feast. That night, however, he took his daughter Leah to sleep with Jacob. In the morning, to his surprise, Jacob discovered that it was Leah!

"What is going on here? Did I not work for you so that I could marry Rachel? Why have you cheated me?" Jacob asked Laban. "It is a local custom that a younger daughter can't be married before her elder sister," Laban assured him. "When the week of the wedding-feast is finished, I'll let you marry Rachel also – if you work seven more years for me."

Jacob agreed, and after the wedding-feast he married Rachel. Jacob went in to sleep with Rachel, too, and he loved her more than Leah. Then he worked for Laban seven more years.

from Genesis, chapter 29, verses 15–30

Above
A bronze sword; the hilt is decorated with sheep heads.

Jacob's two marriages
In the ancient Near East, the husband's family had to pay a "bride-price" to the family of the bride. Jacob paid Laban by working for him for seven years. However, at the wedding a bride was veiled until it was too dark to see who she was, and Laban cheated Jacob by substituting the wrong daughter.

Marriage patterns were flexible in biblical times. Some men, such as Esau and Jacob, had more than one wife; others, such as Isaac and Joseph, had only one. In a nomadic society, the strength of the family was in children. To have many children was considered a special blessing from God.

Some time later Jacob decided to go back to the land of Canaan where he was born. Before he went, he tricked Laban into giving him the best sheep and goats as his wages, and departed a wealthy man. He then settled down in Canaan in the northern hill-country round Bethel and Shechem.

The twelve sons of Jacob
According to the biblical record, the nation of Israel owes its existence to the twelve sons of Jacob by his two wives and the two slave girls whom they presented to Jacob. Typically, each son received a name that expressed the feelings of Leah or Rachel at the time of his birth. Jacob's favorite sons were the two of his favorite wife Rachel. But the biblical writers ultimately vindicate Leah, for her fourth son Judah became the progeniter of the only tribe that has remained identifiable throughout history – the Jews.

A great wedding feast was prepared for Jacob.

Below
Small bone cymbals which were played between the fingers of musicians.

JOSEPH IS SOLD INTO SLAVERY

Jacob lived in Canaan where his father Isaac had stayed. He had many sons. One of them was called Joseph.

When he was seventeen years old, Joseph's job was to watch the sheep and the goats with his brothers. Because the boy had been born when Jacob was very old, Jacob loved him best of all his sons, and made him a decorated coat with long sleeves. Joseph's brothers hated him.

Joseph had dreams that one day all his family would bow down to him. In one, they had all been working in the fields, when their sheaves of wheat had bowed down to his. In another, he claimed he had seen the sun, the moon and eleven stars bowing down to him. Tactlessly, he told his family about these dreams. Even his doting father was exasperated. "What kind of dream is that?" the old man scolded. Then, one day, when Joseph's brothers had taken the flocks to Shechem for pasture, Jacob sent Joseph to see how they were getting on.

Seeing him in the distance, the sons of Jacob plotted together to kill him.

"Here comes that dreamer," they said. "Let's kill him and throw his body into a dried-up well. We can say that a wild animal killed him. So much for his dreams then!" Reuben, however, persuaded them to throw him into the well alive. He planned to come back later to save him and take him home.

While they were eating, they saw a group of Ishmaelite slave-traders travelling to Egypt from Gilead, their camels loaded with resin, myrrh and spices. That gave Judah the idea of selling Joseph into slavery. Some Midianite traders passed and pulled Joseph out of the well. So the sons of Israel sold Joseph to the Ishmaelites for twenty shekels of silver.

Then they killed a goat, dipped Joseph's coat in its blood and took the coat to their father. When he saw it, he said, "Yes! It's Joseph's! A wild animal has killed him." No one could comfort him. "I will go down to the world of the dead grieving for my dead son," he said, and then he wept.

from Genesis, chapter 37, verses 1–35

Ancient tribes

Many of the ancient nations or tribes were named after their founder. The Ishmaelites in this story were the descendants of Ishmael, the son of Abraham and Hagar. Each of the sons of Jacob had a tribe named after them. Reuben and Judah, who play a key role in the saving of Joseph, each founded a tribe.

Storage wells

Lack of water has always been a problem in the hill-country of Palestine. The plentiful rain all falls in six weeks, so it runs off the hillsides in torrents and does little good. The solution is to make little channels which lead rain-water into underground stone pits. These underground pits can be the size of a large room. Many centuries later the prophet Jeremiah was imprisoned in one of these.

The little valley where this story takes place is on the direct trade route from north to south through Palestine, between the East and Egypt. The Ishmaelites carried myrrh from Arabia and spices from India to sell in Egypt.

PHARAOH'S DREAMS

Joseph was taken to Egypt. He became the slave of one of the pharaoh's officers, but was put in prison when the officer's wife accused him of trying to rape her. In prison, he met the pharaoh's baker and wine-steward, and gained their respect when he explained the meanings of their dreams. As Joseph had predicted, the baker was executed, but the wine-steward regained his former job.

Two years later, the pharaoh dreamed he was standing by the Nile. Seven healthy, fat cows came out of the river and started to eat the grass. Then seven thin, bony cows came from the river and ate up the fat cows. The pharaoh woke up, but when he fell asleep again he dreamed that seven ripe, heavy ears of grain were swallowed by seven shrivelled, wind-blasted ears. Then the pharaoh woke again. He realized that he had been dreaming and was worried. The next morning he sent for all his magicians and wise men, but none of them could explain what the dreams meant.

The pharaoh's wine-steward, who had heard what was going on, remembered Joseph and recommended him to the pharaoh. Joseph was brought from prison. He shaved, changed his clothes, and then went before the pharaoh, who described his dreams.

Joseph said to the pharaoh, "Both these dreams mean the same thing: God has shown you what he is going to do. There will be seven years of rich harvests throughout Egypt, but they will be followed by seven years of famine, which will ruin the country. You need to appoint a tactful and intelligent man to collect a fifth of all the crops during the seven good years, and guard them carefully. This will then be a reserve supply for the time of famine."

The pharaoh was delighted. He gave Joseph his gold ring with the royal seal, and made him governor of all Egypt. Joseph had a fine robe and a gold chain to wear, the second royal chariot to ride in, and a guard of honor to run in front of him crying, "Make way! Make way!" The pharaoh married him to Asenath, the daughter of Potiphera, a priest of Heliopolis. In this way, when he was thirty years old, Joseph became famous throughout Egypt.

from Genesis, chapter 41, verses 1–46

Joseph was taken from the dungeon, bathed, and brought before Pharaoh.

Above
An Egyptian wall-painting of ladies holding lotus blossoms.

Dreams foretelling the future
Many ancient peoples regarded dreams as messages from the spirit world to warn about the future. So there were professional interpreters of dreams in Babylon and Egypt.

Joseph rules Egypt
Ancient Egypt was a highly organized country. The pharaoh (this was the king's title) had a large court, with special officials, such as a wine-taster. The governor of all Egypt had a large staff under him, and it would normally take years to work up through this structure.

All agriculture in Egypt was dependent on the annual floods of the River Nile, which brought down fresh, rich soil from the south and spread it over the narrow Egyptian river plains. Water-rationing of the flow of water from the Nile onto surrounding land and teams of farm workers were strictly controlled. Very capable governors would be needed in a famine.

JOSEPH MEETS HIS BROTHERS

The seven good years ended and the seven years of famine began, just as Joseph had said. It spread over all Egypt, and Joseph opened the storehouses and sold the grain. People came from all over the Middle East to buy grain from Joseph, because there was terrible famine everywhere. When Jacob heard that there was grain for sale in Egypt, he said to his sons, "Get moving! Go to Egypt and buy some grain, so we won't starve to death!" So Joseph's ten brothers went to buy grain in Egypt. Only Benjamin, the youngest, stayed at home, because Jacob was afraid he would come to some harm. The brothers went to Joseph and bowed down. He recognized them, but they did not recognize him.

At first Joseph tormented his brothers. He threw them into prison, accusing them of being spies. Then he kept one of them, Simeon, imprisoned as surety, and sent the others back to bring Benjamin to Egypt. When they returned, he gave them a meal – amazing them by seating them at the table according to their ages. Finally, as they set off to return home with the grain, he hid a silver cup in the sacks on Benjamin's donkey. He insisted that Benjamin had stolen it, and should become his slave. The brothers were terrified, and Judah, the eldest, begged to be made a slave instead of his younger brother. "Our father had one son torn to pieces and killed. To lose this son as well would kill him."

Joseph could bear it no longer. He told his servants to leave the room and, when he was alone with his brothers, burst into tears. He wept so loudly that he could be heard all through the house, and even the pharaoh got to know about it! Then Joseph and his brothers embraced, and he sent them back to Palestine to bring their father. Jacob went to Egypt, and it was there that he died. His body was mummified, and Joseph took it back to Palestine to be buried.

from Genesis, chapters 41–45, 50

During the seven years of plenty in Egypt, Joseph stored up the grain in the granaries.

Nomads in time of famine

The borders of Egypt were strictly guarded, and permits given to everyone who passed. In time of drought, nomads used to cross from the Negeb and southern Palestine to seek food in Egypt. Ancient records of these permits still exist. The Scriptures show that Joseph used his influence to gain permission for his brothers to settle in the most fertile part of the country, the delta at the mouth of the Nile. When Jacob died, Joseph took his body back to the ancestral burial-plot to be buried. The burial place of Abraham, Isaac and Jacob is still revered by Jewish and Muslim pilgrims to Hebron.

The Hyksos

The period of Joseph's rule and the settlement of his family in Egypt reflect the period of the Hyksos in Egyptian history. The Hyksos were a nomad people (the name means "shepherd kings") from Asia, who began to infiltrate Egypt about 1720 BC. Gradually they came to dominate Egypt, till they ruled an empire stretching from the south of Egypt to Syria. After 150 years, the Egyptians themselves became strong again and expelled their foreign rulers. Little is known about the Hyksos in Egypt; the Egyptians hated this foreign domination so much that they later attempted to destroy all record of it.

JOSEPH MEETS HIS BROTHERS

The seven good years ended and the seven years of famine began, just as Joseph had said. It spread over all Egypt, and Joseph opened the storehouses and sold the grain. People came from all over the Middle East to buy grain from Joseph, because there was terrible famine everywhere. When Jacob heard that there was grain for sale in Egypt, he said to his sons, "Get moving! Go to Egypt and buy some grain, so we won't starve to death!" So Joseph's ten brothers went to buy grain in Egypt. Only Benjamin, the youngest, stayed at home, because Jacob was afraid he would come to some harm. The brothers went to Joseph and bowed down. He recognized them, but they did not recognize him.

At first Joseph tormented his brothers. He threw them into prison, accusing them of being spies. Then he kept one of them, Simeon, imprisoned as surety, and sent the others back to bring Benjamin to Egypt. When they returned, he gave them a meal – amazing them by seating them at the table according to their ages. Finally, as they set off to return home with the grain, he hid a silver cup in the sacks on Benjamin's donkey. He insisted that Benjamin had stolen it, and should become his slave. The brothers were terrified, and Judah, the eldest, begged to be made a slave instead of his younger brother. "Our father had one son torn to pieces and killed. To lose this son as well would kill him."

Joseph could bear it no longer. He told his servants to leave the room and, when he was alone with his brothers, burst into tears. He wept so loudly that he could be heard all through the house, and even the pharaoh got to know about it! Then Joseph and his brothers embraced, and he sent them back to Palestine to bring their father. Jacob went to Egypt, and it was there that he died. His body was mummified, and Joseph took it back to Palestine to be buried.

from Genesis, chapters 41–45, 50

During the seven years of plenty in Egypt, Joseph stores up the grain in the granaries.

Nomads in time of famine

The borders of Egypt were strictly guarded, and permits given to everyone who passed. In time of drought, nomads used to cross from the Negeb and southern Palestine to seek food in Egypt. Ancient records of these permits still exist. The Scriptures show that Joseph used his influence to gain permission for his brothers to settle in the most fertile part of the country, the delta at the mouth of the Nile. When Jacob died, Joseph took his body back to the ancestral burial-plot to be buried. The burial place of Abraham, Isaac and Jacob is still revered by Jewish and Muslim pilgrims to Hebron.

The Hyksos

The period of Joseph's rule and the settlement of his family in Egypt reflect the period of the Hyksos in Egyptian history. The Hyksos were a nomad people (the name means "shepherd kings") from Asia, who began to infiltrate Egypt about 1720 BC. Gradually they came to dominate Egypt, till they ruled an empire stretching from the south of Egypt to Syria. After 150 years, the Egyptians themselves became strong again and expelled their foreign rulers. Little is known about the Hyksos in Egypt; the Egyptians hated this foreign domination so much that they later attempted to destroy all record of it.

The Baby in the Bulrushes

When he was too big to keep hidden from the Egyptians, Moses was put into a basket among the reeds at the river's edge.

In time, Joseph and all his brothers died, but the Israelite people had many children and became very numerous. Then, however, there came to the throne a new pharaoh, who did not remember what Joseph had done for Egypt. He was afraid of the Israelites, because there were so many of them.

So the Egyptians enslaved the Israelites and set them to build the cities of Pithom and Rameses. The more they were oppressed, the more the Israelites grew in number. Finally, the pharaoh ordered Shiphrah and Puah (the two women who acted as midwives for the Israelites) to "take every new-born Israelite boy and throw him into the River Nile".

About this time, an Israelite couple from the tribe of Levi had a son. He was a fine boy, and his mother hid him until he grew too big to keep secret. Then she made a basket out of reeds, covered it with tar to make it watertight, put the baby in it and hid it among the reeds at the river's edge. His elder sister waited a little way away to see what would happen.

That day, the pharaoh's daughter came with her servants to bathe in the river. As they walked along the bank, she noticed the basket in the tall reeds. When she opened it, she found the baby boy inside. He was crying, and her heart was touched.

His sister stepped forward and offered to find a wet-nurse for the child; the princess agreed, so his sister brought Moses' own mother to be his nurse! When he had grown older, pharaoh's daughter adopted Moses, and brought him up as an Egyptian prince.

from Exodus, chapter 1 to chapter 2, verse 10

The persecution of the Hebrews

When the family of Jacob came into Egypt, that country was ruled by a foreign race, the Hyksos, who dominated Egypt for 200 years. It is little wonder, then, that the Hebrews received special treatment as another foreign people. When the Egyptians grew strong again and drove out the Hyksos, the new pharaohs hated the Israelites, and began to oppress them.

The pharaoh at the time of Moses was Rameses II, one of the most powerful of all the pharaohs. He ruled Egypt for more than sixty years, 1290–1224 BC. He was responsible for building the cities where the Hebrews labored as slaves. The royal government in Egypt controlled every kind of activity closely, in such a way that it would be easy to victimize a particular group of people like the Hebrews.

The royal palace was near the sea, in the delta of the River Nile, where the great river divides into several different streams. These muddy streams flow quite slowly; it would not be dangerous either to float the baby's basket or for the princess to come to bathe.

Moses, prince of the Egyptians

At this time Egyptian influence spread to the north-east, into Palestine and Asia. Egyptian garrisons were stationed all over this territory in strongholds. The careful Egyptian administration needed to write letters to the local rulers of these territories. Many languages were in use, and the Egyptians trained scribes and translators to work in the administration.

Some languages used were of the same group as Moses' own language, Hebrew, which was quite different from Egyptian. This adoptive son of the princess may well have been trained as a scribe to write letters in his own language for the pharaoh. There was a strict training, with a clear code of good behavior. For Moses to succeed he would have had to dress and behave like other Egyptian noblemen.

Overleaf

The enslaved Hebrews labored on the pharaoh's new cities. They made bricks by forming mud in wooden moulds.

When he had grown to be a man, Moses went to see what was happening to his own people in the labor-gangs. He realized how badly they were oppressed. When he saw one Egyptian strike down an Israelite slave, Moses looked about to check there was no one watching, and then he killed the Egyptian, and hid the body in the sand.

Next day Moses returned. Two Israelites were fighting, and Moses tried to stop them. "Why are you hitting a fellow-Israelite?" he asked the one in the wrong. "Who made you our ruler and judge?" replied the man. "I suppose you're going to kill me now, just as you killed the Egyptian." Then Moses was scared, because he knew that the pharaoh would find out what he had done. And indeed, when the pharaoh found out, he ordered Moses to be put to death.

Moses ran away to live with a Midianite chieftain named Jethro. One day, as he watched Jethro's flocks at Mount Horeb, the messenger of the Lord appeared to him in a burning bush. Although the bush was on fire, it wasn't destroyed by the flames. Then God said, "Moses! I have seen my people's troubles in Egypt. I will send you to the pharaoh, so you can bring my people, the children of Israel, out of Egypt."

"What shall I say if they ask me: 'What is your God's name?'" Moses asked. God replied, "I AM WHO I AM. Tell them, 'Yahweh (I AM) has sent me.'"

from Exodus, chapter 2, verse 11 to chapter 3, verse 14

Above
Moses grew up as an Egyptian.

Slave-gangs
Slaves were everywhere in Egypt, employed in every kind of work. The Scriptures tell of the Hebrews engaged in building cities. They also worked in the mines of the Sinai peninsula, for Hebrew letters have been found scratched on rocks at ancient mines.

Moses' flight
Moses fled to Midian and became a shepherd like his ancestors before him. Midian is in the desert of Sinai, to the east of Egypt, across what is now the Suez Canal. He married the daughter of Jethro. However, he was not allowed to settle down as a shepherd, and his experience of God at the burning bush changed his whole life and the life of his people.

The Burning Bush
In the Scriptures, God's presence is often made known by fire. The Lord therefore made his presence known to Moses through the burning bush. He knew that he was called to free his people from slavery and lead them out of Egypt. As a guarantee of his special favor and friendship, God made known to Moses his own personal name, Yahweh. Till then he had been known only as the God of the ancestors, "the God of Abraham", or "the Fear of Isaac", or "the Strength of Jacob". To reveal your name to someone is always a sign of trust and friendship. Now God entrusts this sign of favor to Moses, to encourage and strengthen him for his task.

Moses' Reluctance
Not wanting to take the awsome task of leading the Israelites out of Egypt, Moses raised at least four objections in his encounter with the Lord. The Lord answered each objection, promising to be with him and providing Moses' brother Aaron as his assistant.

THE PLAGUES OF EGYPT

Right
The second plague caused frogs to swarm from the canals, lakes and rivers over the land.

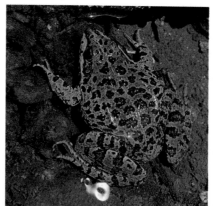

The Lord said to Moses, "Watch what I am going to do to the pharaoh. He won't just tell you to leave – he'll drive you out! I have heard the groans of the Israelites who are the Egyptians' slaves, and I have remembered my contract with them. Go and tell the pharaoh he must let the Israelites leave Egypt."

Moses, however, answered, "My words are not enough. The pharaoh won't listen."

Then the Lord said, "Aaron your brother shall be your spokesman. Tell him everything I tell you, and he will command pharaoh to let the Israelites go. The pharaoh will be stubborn, but I will cause terrifying disasters, until the Egyptians realize that I am the Lord, and let the Israelites go to their own country."

Moses and Aaron did as the Lord commanded.

Disaster after disaster struck Egypt. The river turned blood-red. There were plagues of frogs, mosquitoes, flies. A sickness killed their domestic animals and they suffered boils, a hailstorm, locusts and a darkness which covered the land. Finally all the first-born died.

from Exodus, chapters 6–10

The ten plagues

The ten disasters listed in the biblical record are all demonstrations of God's power in favor of his people, attempts to persuade the pharaoh to let them go. These plagues gradually increase in intensity – from the mere irritation of impure water and the land filled with frogs, gnats, and flies, to the destruction of many crops and livestock, to the final plague of the death of the first-born male descendants in Egypt.

Some of the plagues could have a natural explanation. The Nile River turning to blood may describe an unusually large annual flood in which the river was so full of rich, red earth that it resembled blood. The flies may be related to mounds of dead, decaying frogs. The darkness could well be a ferocious sandstorm; at some times of the year in the deserts of Egypt the air is so full of sand and dust that an eerie darkness hangs over the whole land. But whatever explanations we may give, for Moses and the Israelites the miraculous element came not so much in the plague itself as in the fact that each one came as a result of the word of the Lord, spoken through Moses.

God used every threat to persuade the pharaoh to "release the children of Israel." Each time after the pharaoh agreed, he backed down from his promise. Even when the Israelites finally went, he gave chase to make them return.

Below
In the eighth plague locusts were so numerous that the ground could not be seen.

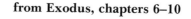

God commanded the Israelites to paint the doorposts and the lintels of their houses with the blood of a sacrificial lamb.

Despite all the disasters, pharaoh still refused to let the Israelites leave.

Finally, the Lord said to Moses, "I have just one more punishment for the pharaoh of Egypt and his people. After that he will let you go – indeed, he will beg you to leave.

"Tell all the Israelites that on the tenth day of this month the man of each household must choose a lamb or a young goat. It must be a one-year-old lamb or goat without blemish. If any family is too poor, it can share an animal with the next-door neighbors. On the fourteenth day of the month, in the evening, all the Israelite families shall kill their lambs. They shall paint some of its blood on to the doorposts and the lintels of their houses. That night, they shall roast and eat the meat, together with unleavened bread and bitter herbs. You must eat it all, and burn all the left-overs. You must eat it quickly, with your coat tucked into your belt, your sandals on your feet, and your walking-staff in your hand.

"This is the Passover festival of the Lord. For on that night I will pass through the land of Egypt, and I will kill every first-born man and animal. I will punish the gods of Egypt, for I am the Lord. The blood on your houses will be your special sign, and when I see the blood I will pass over you – no plague will harm you when I strike the land of Egypt.

"However, you must always remember this day, and make it one of your Laws for ever, to celebrate it as a festival for the Lord."

from Exodus, chapters 11 and 12

The Passover

Israel's later history, especially in the prophets and the psalms, constantly referred to Israel's exodus from Egypt as God's most significant saving deed in their history. They continually referred to God as "the one who brought them out of the land of Egypt." It was this event that initiated the fulfillment of God's promise to give Abraham's descendants the land of Canaan.

This saving act of God was remembered in the annual festival of Passover, which was instituted at this time and continues to this day in Judaism. The youngest child in a Jewish family asks the question, "What do these things mean?" The response is: "The unleavened bread reminds us of the hastily prepared bread for the journey. The bitter herbs remind us of the bitter years of slavery in Egypt. The salt water reminds us of the tears which were shed. The shank bone represents the young lamb which was killed and whose blood was smeared on the lintels to save the first-born Israelite sons from death."

Christianity adopted the symbolism of the Passover by viewing Jesus as the Passover Lamb (he was crucified during the Passover) and by seeing Israel's redemption from Egypt as a symbol of God's salvation in Christ.

AT THE SEA OF REEDS

After the death of all the first-born on the night of the Passover, the pharaoh ordered the Israelites to leave the country. They filled all their pots and pans with unleavened bread-dough, and set off through the desert. The Lord guided them by means of a column of cloud by day and a column of fire by night.

When the pharaoh was told, however, that the Israelites had escaped, he and his officials changed their minds. The pharaoh called for his war-chariot, mobilized his army, and set out.

When they saw the Egyptian army marching towards them, the terrified Israelites said to Moses, "Have they run out of graves in Egypt? Is that why you brought us out here into the desert to die? It would have been better to have remained slaves than to die here!"

Moses said to the people, "Don't panic. Pull yourselves together! Today you will see the Lord save you." The column of cloud came between the camp of the Egyptians and the escaping Israelites. Moses stretched out his hand over the sea, and the Lord drove back the sea with a strong east wind. The sea-bed was exposed, and the Israelites crossed over on dry ground.

The Egyptian chariots tried to follow, but their wheels became stuck. Then the Lord told Moses to stretch out his hand over the sea again. The waters returned and drowned the Egyptian army.

from Exodus, chapters 12–14

Above
The Israelites went into the sea on dry ground and crossed over.

The miracle of the sea
The crossing of the Red Sea is the final demonstration of God's saving power in the exodus. As with the ten plagues, the miracle lies in this act of salvation, in that the Israelites, through the Lord's intervention, were able to cross over safely and the pursuing Egyptians were not.

The Sea of Reeds
Nobody knows where the Sea of Reeds is. The similarity between the words "Reeds" and "Red" exists only in English. It is not the Red Sea. Many scholars think it refers to the marshy sections at the southern end of Lake Manzaleh, north of the Gulf of Suez. Some scholars suggest that what possibly happened was that a strong wind lowered the water level as the Israelites crossed over. The wind then subsided and the detachment of Egyptian cavalry which was pursuing them got bogged down in the mud. The horses perished, the riders could not swim and so were drowned when the wind subsided and the water rose again.

A song of victory
Safely on the other side, the Israelites sang a song of praise to the Lord, which is recorded in Exodus 15:1–21. Military victories in the ancient world frequently became a subject of the poets and singers.

Prominent in the singing of victory songs were women. In the biblical text, Miriam (Moses' sister) took a tambourine in her hand and led all the Israelite women in singing and dancing. Such excitement is understandable, for prominent in military defeats was the rape and enslavement of conquered women.

The chariots of the pursuing Egyptians became clogged with mud and they drowned.

Overleaf
When Moses delayed coming down from the mountain the people made a golden calf.

54

AT MOUNT SINAI

hree months after leaving Egypt, the Israelites set up camp at the foot of Mount Sinai. Moses went up the mountain to meet with God. The Lord called to him, "I am going to make a contract with you." Moses went down to the people and told them what the Lord had said.

Two days later, there was thunder and lightning and dense cloud on the mountain. All the people trembled. Mount Sinai was wrapped in smoke. Then God spoke,

"I am the Lord your God, who took you away from the land of Egypt, and from your life as slaves there.

Don't worship any other gods but me. Don't make idols or statues. Don't bow down to such things or worship them. Don't use the name of the Lord your God in the wrong way.

Remember to keep the sabbath day special, set apart for God. You can work for six days, but the seventh day is a rest-day dedicated to the Lord. The Lord blessed the sabbath day and made it holy, because he himself created the universe in six days, and rested on the seventh. Honor your father and mother, so that you may live a long life in the land I will give you.
Don't kill.
Don't commit adultery.
Don't steal.
Don't give false testimony about others.
Don't envy the possessions of others."

Moses returned to Mount Sinai and stayed there so long that the Israelites thought he was dead. They made a gold calf and worshipped it. The Lord was angry, but Moses pleaded for the Israelites.

from Exodus, chapters 19, 20 and 32

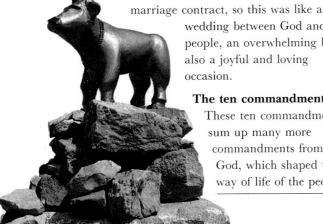

Below
Aaron told the people to take off their gold rings and he made them all into an image of a calf.

Meeting with God
The moment of this meeting with God on Mount Sinai was the crucial moment in the history of Israel. The Israelites looked back on it ever afterwards as the moment when their nation had come into being.

Before then, God had made a contract with an individual, Abraham, and had promised to make him father of a great nation. Now the contract was made with the nation as a whole. The Israelites regarded it as a marriage contract, so this was like a wedding between God and his people, an overwhelming but also a joyful and loving occasion.

The ten commandments
These ten commandments sum up many more commandments from God, which shaped the way of life of the people of Israel. Any contract has conditions attached to it, and obedience to these laws was the condition of the marriage contract between God and his people.

Many of the same laws about behavior, honesty, respect for other people and their rights, have been found in other law codes of the Near East. One of these is the law code of Hammurabi, king of Babylon (1728–1686 BC). These other law codes, however, do not contain parallels to Israelite religious laws. Especially unusual was the prohibition of any idols or images. The Israelites always accepted that the Lord was too great to be represented by any carving or statue.

The Lord said to Moses, "Move on and take the people who you brought with you from Egypt. Go to the land which I promised to give to Abraham. I will send an angel before you and drive out your enemies. Keep on going until you reach the land flowing with milk and honey." Moses said, "Let me see your glory." The Lord replied: "You cannot see my face, for no man can see me and live. Stand in this cleft in the rock, and I will cover you with my hand as I pass by; then I shall take away my hand, and you may see my back. You must not look at my face."

Then the Lord gave Moses the Law a second time, carved on two tablets of stone. When Moses returned from Mount Sinai, his face shone so brightly that none of the people dared to look at him.

Moses had a special place made for the people to go and worship God in a tent of meeting which he pitched away from the camp. The Lord had revealed instructions about this structure: its tent and covering and the Ark, containing the Law, with its mercy seat. He put the tent of meeting on the north side of the tabernacle and arranged the lamps and screens. He anointed Aaron and his sons as priests.

Then the glory of the the Lord filled the tent of meeting – a cloud covered the tabernacle by day and at night it glowed with fire. Whenever the cloud left the tabernacle the Israelites would set out on the next stage of their journey.

In this way, Moses led them in the desert for forty years. The Israelites kept God's Laws and he provided for them.

from Exodus, chapters 33–40

Left
Small groups of people were able to survive by wandering with their flocks in the desert.

The way through the desert

The group of fugitives led by Moses survived all the trials and dangers of the desert for forty years. During this time, they became a nation successful in battle. They carried with them everywhere the tent of meeting or tabernacle containing the Ark.

The tabernacle

Many ancient peoples represented the presence of their god through an idol or some image. It was central to the beliefs of Moses and his predecessors that God could never be represented by a man-made image. Instead, the presence of God was represented by the tabernacle which contained the Ark. In this Ark was a copy of God's Law, in which the worship of idols was expressly forbidden.

Later when the Jews settled in the land of Canaan, and were tempted to worship idols like the other nations, the great prophets pointed back to the desert years as the model of pure worship.

God's care

The historians of Israel saw that their ancestors had been specially protected by the Lord. The biblical text records how God provided food and water for them in areas where their was no food and how he protected them from danger.

Overleaf
Moses led the Israelites for forty years in the desert.

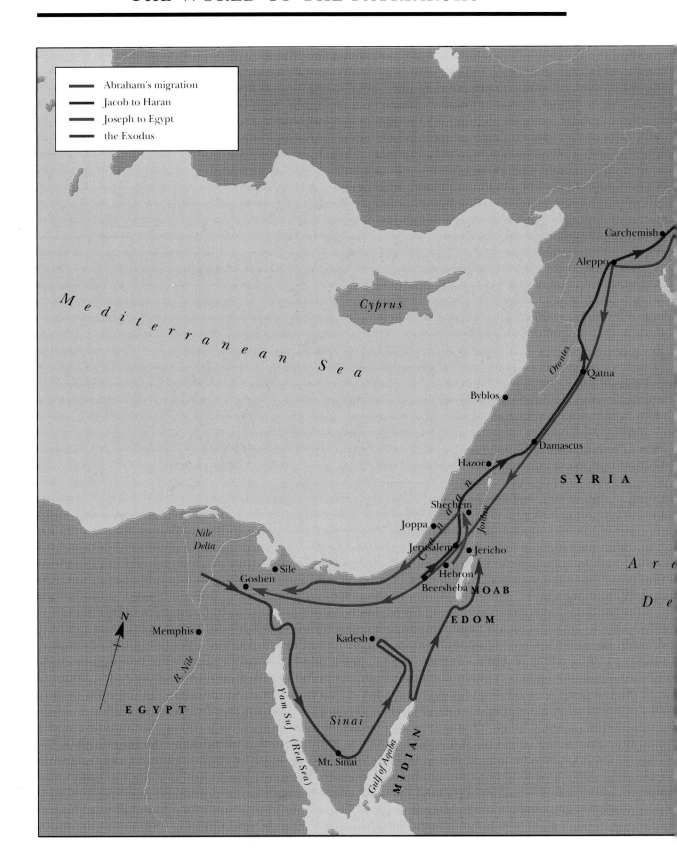

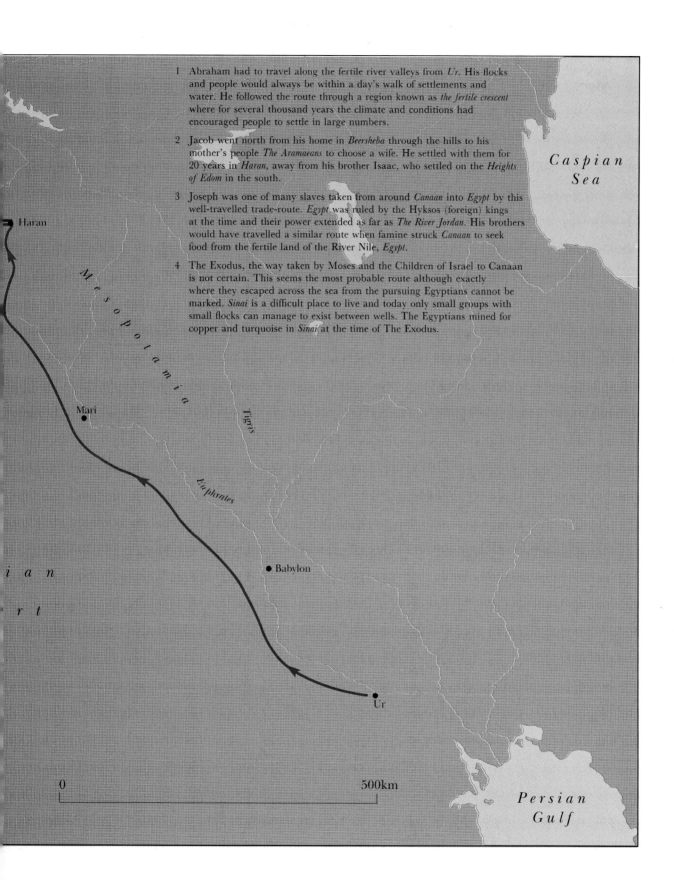

1   Abraham had to travel along the fertile river valleys from *Ur*. His flocks and people would always be within a day's walk of settlements and water. He followed the route through a region known as *the fertile crescent* where for several thousand years the climate and conditions had encouraged people to settle in large numbers.

2   Jacob went north from his home in *Beersheba* through the hills to his mother's people *The Aramaeans* to choose a wife. He settled with them for 20 years in *Haran*, away from his brother Isaac, who settled on the *Heights of Edom* in the south.

3   Joseph was one of many slaves taken from around *Canaan* into *Egypt* by this well-travelled trade-route. *Egypt* was ruled by the Hyksos (foreign) kings at the time and their power extended as far as *The River Jordan*. His brothers would have travelled a similar route when famine struck *Canaan* to seek food from the fertile land of the River Nile, *Egypt*.

4   The Exodus, the way taken by Moses and the Children of Israel to Canaan is not certain. This seems the most probable route although exactly where they escaped across the sea from the pursuing Egyptians cannot be marked. *Sinai* is a difficult place to live and today only small groups with small flocks can manage to exist between wells. The Egyptians mined for copper and turquoise in *Sinai* at the time of The Exodus.

Haran

Mesopotamia

Mari

Tigris

Euphrates

● Babylon

i a n

r t

Ur

Caspian Sea

0   500km

Persian Gulf

When Moses died, the Lord spoke to his second-in-command, Joshua, the son of Nun. He said, "Moses my servant is dead. Arise! Lead my people across the River Jordan into the land that I am going to give you. Every place the sole of your foot treads upon, I shall give to you. No one will be able to defeat you all the days of your life.

"Never stop telling people about the Laws Moses laid down for you. Think about them day and night, so that you will be able to take care to obey them – for then you shall be wealthy and successful. Have I not commanded you? Be strong and brave! Do not be frightened or dismayed, for the Lord your God is with you wherever you go."

from Joshua, chapter 1, verses 1–9

Above
A sling is a simple and effective weapon.

The formation of a people

The Bible begins with the story of creation and the dependence of all creatures on God, and the struggle of the human race against the growing problem of sin and evil. Then comes the accounts of Abraham, Isaac and Jacob, who were wandering nomads, protected by their God, the Lord, as they shepherded their flocks on the edges of the civilized areas of Canaan. Because of a great drought, they took refuge in the rich Nile delta, where they were later enslaved by the Egyptians. Finally Moses led them out from slavery, in an escape which owed everything to the intervention of the Lord.

Moses

Moses saw the Promised Land, but he never entered it. The Scriptures say this was a punishment for one act of disobedience of Moses and his brother Aaron. On one of the many occasions when the people of Israel, wearied of their suffering and in desperate need for water, complained to Moses and Aaron and blamed them for making them suffer, the brothers pleaded to the Lord. The Lord told him to speak to a rock and it would pour out water. Moses momentarily disbelieved and struck the rock twice. As a punishment, the Lord declared that Moses and his brother would never achieve their final goal of entering Canaan. This was to be left to their successors.

Joshua

Joshua first comes into the story as one of twelve spies sent by Moses to reconnoiter Canaan from the south. They came back to report that it was a land flowing with milk and honey. Ten of them stressed that the inhabitants were so gigantic that they themselves felt like grasshoppers. So the people were scared and refused to obey Moses' instructions to advance. Joshua and Caleb, however, encouraged the people to advance in the name of the Lord. This willingness to trust the Lord stood Joshua in good stead when Moses appointed him as his successor and gave him authority over the people to complete his task.

The entry into Canaan

What guided Joshua during his term of leadership were the laws of Moses, which Moses had introduced in the desert. These laws, developed for a nomadic people, became the foundation of the religious and social life of the people as they settled in the new land.

Below
Soldiers carried many different weapons. Archers, slingers, and spear-throwers were all part of an army.

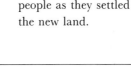

Joshua commanded the Israelites' leaders to go through the camp and give the order, "Prepare some food. In three days' time you are going to cross over the River Jordan to conquer the land that the Lord is giving you."

Then Joshua summoned the tribes of Reuben and Gad, and the half-tribe of Manasseh. He said, "I know that Moses decided that you would settle here on the east side of the River Jordan. You can leave your wives, children and cattle here, but your brave soldiers are needed to help the invasion. You will be the first to cross over the River Jordan, and you cannot return until the Israelites have conquered the land which the Lord is giving to them."

To this they replied, "We will do everything you command, and we will go wherever you send us. We will obey you just as we obeyed Moses, and we will put to death anybody who disobeys your orders. Be strong and brave!"

from Joshua, chapter 1, verses 10–18

Right
At first the Israelites lacked horses and chariots to make war against the people they found in Canaan. Often their commanders used mules and donkeys.

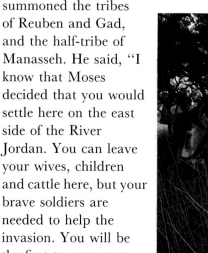
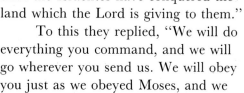

Crossing the River Jordan

The Book of Joshua tells how the tribes crossed the dry river-bed. There was a miraculous crossing of water at the end of the forty years of wandering, just as at the beginning, when they crossed the Reed Sea, led by Moses. The River Jordan is surrounded by large hillocks, eroded into strange shapes by the wind. Sometimes these collapse into the river. Several times in recorded history the river has been completely blocked by rockfalls and earthquakes, most recently in 1927. It may be that such a blockage occurred opportunely for the Hebrews.

As with the ten plagues and the crossing of the Sea of Reeds, the miracle in this story is not the stopping of the waters of the Jordan per se, but the fact that it occurred by the word of the Lord as spoken through his servant Joshua.

The cohesion of the Israelites

As the Israelites entered into Canaan, what held them together as a nation was their loyalty to the Lord and his Law. They were all partners in the contract that God had made in the desert with Moses and the people at Mount Sinai. This contract had been renewed on the eastern bank of the Jordan, and it was later renewed again by Joshua in the great ceremony of the Passover at Shechem.

RAHAB AND THE SPIES

Joshua sent two spies into Canaan. "Go and look over the land, especially the city of Jericho," he told them. So they went to Jericho, where they stayed at the house of a woman named Rahab.

When the king of Jericho discovered that the Israelites had sent spies to check out the land, he sent some soldiers to Rahab's house, commanding her to hand over her guests. Rahab, however, had hidden the two men under a pile of flax on the roof of her house. She said, "Some strangers did come to my house, but I don't know where from, and they left when it grew dark, before the city gates closed." The soldiers went out and searched the countryside as far as the fords of the River Jordan. As soon as they left, the city gates were shut.

Rahab went up to the two spies. "I know that the Lord has promised you this land. Everyone here is terrified of fighting you. We realize that your God, the Lord, is God of heaven and earth. I have saved you. Please promise that you will save my family," she said.

Rahab's house was built into the city wall, so she was able to open a window and let the spies escape by lowering them down on a rope. "Tie a bright red piece of cloth in your window, and we guarantee that no one in your house will be killed," they told her.

The spies hid for three days, until the soldiers had given up searching for them. Then they crossed back over the River Jordan to return to Joshua. "Truly the Lord has given us this land; everybody is terrified of us," they reported.

from Joshua, chapter 2

Left
Rahab of Jericho.

Jericho

At first human beings subsisted by hunting and this meant they were always on the move. Then some of them left their nomadic life and began to settle down, grow their own crops and build houses. Jericho claims to be the oldest city in the world. Certainly the finest building of the Stone Age is Jericho's circular tower, 6 metres high, built about 8000 BC. It has the ideal climate for agriculture: built in the Jordan Valley, 300 metres below sea-level, it is sunny and warm even in winter. Water is provided by a plentiful spring, which produces over 4500 litres of water a minute. It may well have been here that agriculture first began.

The old city is the perfect example of a "Tell" (Arabic for "hill"). In Palestine many of the cities, including Jericho, were built of mud-brick. In time, these houses fell down or were destroyed, and the next generation merely built on top of the ruins. So the hill gets higher and higher. Over twenty separate levels of occupation have been traced at Jericho.

The city walls were several feet thick. In many places these walls can still be seen, the mud-bricks welded together by a sort of mortar. Often houses were built into the city wall: it meant there was one less wall of the house to build, and it gave extra strength to the fortifications of the city.

Rahab is described in the Scriptures as a prostitute. So, it was clever of the two spies to go and stay with her, as they would not be noticed among the other men Rahab entertained.

The two spies escaped from Jericho, at dusk, lowering themselves by a rope from a window.

THE WALLS OF JERICHO COME DOWN

The people of Jericho closed the city gates. No one could leave or enter the city. However, the Lord said to Joshua, "Watch! I will give you Jericho, its king and all its mighty warriors. March round the city. Take with you the Ark in which the Law is kept. The priests must walk in front of it, carrying their shofar horns. Do this once a day for six days, and on the seventh day, march round the city seven times, while the priests sound the shofar horns. Then, as they give one long, final blast on the shofar horn, everybody must give a great shout. The city walls will collapse, and you will be able to attack."

For six days the Israelites followed the Lord's orders. On the seventh day, the Israelites woke up early, and marched round the city seven times, while the priests sounded the shofar horns. After the seventh circuit, Joshua commanded, "Shout, for the Lord has given us the city!" So the shofar horns were blown, and the people gave a great shout, and the walls fell down. Then the Israelite army ran up the mound into the city and captured it. They killed all the people, cattle, sheep and donkeys, and looted the silver, gold, bronze and iron. Then they set fire to the houses and razed the city to the ground.

On Joshua's orders, however, Rahab and her relatives were spared because she had hidden the spies he had sent to Jericho.

from Joshua, chapter 6, verses 1–25

Above
A priest sounds the shofar horn.

The capture of Jericho

The capture of Jericho is not described as a military operation but as a religious procession. The shofar horns are rams' horns, used by the priests for sacred purposes. Still today they are used to sound the beginning and end of the sabbath.

The Ark was a portable box carried only by the priests, containing the tablets of stone on which were written the Ten Commandments. It was the symbol of God's presence among his people, and was carried at the head of the column in the desert and here as they advanced into battle.

For the Israelites, numbers had a special significance. The number seven is a sacred number, the number of perfection. So everything about the preparations for the capture of the city is designed to show that the Israelites captured this first city in Canaan not by their own efforts but by God's own work and patronage.

The destruction of the Canaanites

The extermination of the citizens of Jericho and everything they owned constitutes a perplexing moral problem in the Bible. Jericho was the Israelites' first conquest in the land God promised them. What happened there was to be symbolic of the entire conquest. God commanded, therefore, that everything in this city belonged to him and nothing was to be taken for personal use. There were only two ways to ensure the fulfillment of this command: everything was either to be destroyed or given for use in the tabernacle. This policy did not apply, however, to the other cities taken by the Israelites.

As soon as the people heard the trumpets they gave a great shout and the walls of Jericho fell down.

Overleaf
At Gideon's signal the Israelites held up their torches on the edge of the enemy's camp. The Midianites panicked and fled.

Below
A defender of Jericho.

GIDEON

The Israelites disobeyed the Lord, so he allowed them to be defeated by a local tribe called the Midianites. They were so cruel that the Israelites had to hide in caves, dens and fortified places in the hills. Every summer the Midianites and their allies attacked and destroyed the crops and herds, leaving nothing to eat. Their warriors, cattle and camels were beyond counting – like a swarm of locusts – and they stripped the land bare as they passed through. So the people cried out to the Lord for help.

In the village of Ophrah lived a brave and mighty man named Gideon. The Lord ordered him, "Go and devote your strength to rescuing Israel from the Midianites." Gideon destroyed the local shrine to Baal, and prepared to fight the Midianites. He took the name Jerubaal (which means "let Baal defend

Below
A soldier of the Midianites who had oppressed the Israelites.

himself"). Twenty thousand Israelites volunteered for his army, but he chose only the 300 toughest men. Then he set out against the Midianites.

Gideon divided the 300 men into three groups, giving each man a shofar horn and an empty water-jar with a lamp inside it. Just after midnight, he and his men crept up to the edge of the Midianites' camp. Suddenly, on Gideon's signal, the Israelites blew their shofar horns, broke the jars, held up the torches in their left hands, and shouted, "For the Lord and for Gideon."

The Midianite army panicked and fled. In the confusion, the enemy soldiers even killed each other. Then the whole Israelite nation took up weapons. They drove the Midianites from their land.

from Judges, chapters 6–7

Left
One of the 300 chosen by Gideon to defeat the numerous Midianite army.

The Israelites in Canaan
The Israelites remained quite weak and vulnerable in Canaan. They could not capture the great cities like Jerusalem. They had no chariots, so they could not control the rich plains where chariot warfare was possible. They had to keep to the hill-country, where plowing and agriculture were made difficult by the stony ground.

The Midianites came from the great plains on the far side of the Jordan. Their strength lay in their war-camels. This is the first mention of camels being tamed and used.

In warfare they became particularly important; horses dislike their smell so much that they will not charge at them.

The pattern of Israelite history
The period of the judges began a pattern that repeated itself over and over in Israel's history – right to the time when Jerusalem was sacked by Nebuchadnezzar and his troops, and the Israelites had been taken into captivity in Babylon. 1. The people were unfaithful to the Lord and failed to keep his law. 2. The Lord arranged for them to be punished by attack from the outside. 3. The people returned to the Lord and cried out for help. 4. The Lord delivered them from slavery through a great warrior.

SAMSON

Yet again the Israelites disobeyed the Lord, and they were conquered by a neighboring nation called the Philistines. A "judge" called Samson led a guerrilla war against the invaders. He was a Nazirite; that is, he had dedicated himself to God (the sign of this was that he promised never to cut his hair). Once he killed a lion with his bare hands. Another time the Philistines bound him with ropes, but he broke free and killed large numbers of them with the jaw-bone of a donkey.

The Philistine kings persuaded Delilah, one of their women whom Samson loved, to trick him into telling her the secret of his strength. She kept on badgering him until he told her, "I would be like any ordinary man if I had my hair cut off." Delilah lulled him to sleep, and had his head shaved. Samson's strength left him. Then she called out mockingly, "Samson! The Philistines are here!" Waking up, he said, "I will go out and defeat them, as I have always done before" – he hadn't realized that the Lord had deserted him. The Philistines captured him, gouged his eyes out, and sent him to prison. His hair started to grow again.

One day, the five kings of the Philistines met to celebrate the festival of Dagon. "Our god has helped us to capture Samson," they shouted. "Let's have some fun; let's bring out Samson to entertain us!" They stood him between the two pillars which held up the roof, and mocked him. Samson asked the boy who led him out to show him where the pillars were. The inside of the house was full of men and women watching and jeering at Samson.

Then Samson prayed, "O the Lord, remember me and strengthen me just this once, so I can have my revenge on the men who took my eyes." He grabbed the two central pillars of the building and pushed against them with all his might. The building came crashing down, killing the five kings and everyone else.

from Judges, chapters 14–16

Above
A Canaanite stele.

Overleaf
Samson pushed on the central pillars of the building and brought down the roof on the Philistines.

The Philistines

The Philistines arrived in Canaan soon after Joshua and the people of Israel. They came originally from the area we now call Turkey. After sailing as far south as Egypt they settled on the eastern Mediterranean coastal plain in 1198 BC. It is from their name that this coastal plain received the name "Palestine". For a long time they troubled the Israelites, and gradually advanced into the Israelite hill-country. They were better organized (until the Israelites had their own king), and they were richer (through their trade across the Mediterranean). They had very fine pottery. Above all, they had iron. This gave them stronger weapons than the bronze weapons of the Israelites, and also more effective plows. The Israelites gradually acquired iron implements, but the Philistines prevented them setting up iron-working forges. If anything needed repair, it had to be taken to the Philistines.

Samson the Judge

Samson is called a "judge", but he does not seem to have done much judging! To some of the "judges" of Israel the people brought their difficulties and problems for judgment, but they were more military leaders and champions than legal officials. They led the Israelites to drive out the foreigners who invaded and oppressed them. Samson was enabled by his strength to annoy, injure and kill the Philistines.

Below
Philistine pots decorated with birds and animals.

THE CALL OF SAMUEL

While he was very young, a boy called Samuel was taken by his mother Hannah to the sanctuary of the Lord at Shiloh. There he helped Eli, the high priest. Eli's sons and family were particularly wicked, and openly helped themselves to the offerings which people took to the sanctuary.

When Eli was high priest, few people had visions or prophecies from the Lord. Eli was virtually blind, and the young boy Samuel looked after him. Samuel slept in the Holy Place of the sanctuary, in front of the Ark in which the Law was kept.

One night, the lamp of perpetual light was burning in the Holy Place. It was still not yet dawn, and the Lord called, "Samuel! Samuel!" The boy ran to Eli. "You called for me. Here I am," he said. Eli, however, answered, "I didn't call you. Go back to bed."

It happened a second time. When the Lord called a third time, Samuel went to Eli again. Eli realized that the Lord was calling the boy, so he told him, "Go back to bed. If God calls again, say, 'the Lord! Your servant is listening.' "

"Samuel! Samuel!" The Lord called as before, but this time Samuel answered, "Your servant is listening." The Lord said, "I am going to do a thing in Israel so terrible that everyone who hears about it will be shocked, and I am going to punish Eli's family severely."

from 1 Samuel, chapter 3

Left
A light was always left burning in the sanctuary.

Prophets and seers

Samuel was the last of the "judges" of Israel and the first of the prophets in the Scriptures. He is also called a "seer," from the clear vision given him by the Lord. The prophets were spokespersons for the Lord, introducing their messages by "Thus say the Lord." They were called to be the messengers of the Lord. They acted as the "conscience" of the Israelites, often rebuking them for their unfaithfulness and sins, sometimes threatening them with disaster if they did not improve. Later their sayings were written down in the Scriptures.

False prophets

Some people appeared to be prophets, and served several of the kings. These false prophets would tell the king what he wanted to hear, and then say it was God's message. It was not always easy to tell who were genuinely guided by the Spirit of God and who were false prophets. There were other groups of prophets, "brotherhoods," who claimed that the Spirit of the Lord led them to sing and dance in his praise.

The sanctuary at Shiloh

There were a number of shrines up and down the country where the Lord could be worshipped. Some of them had already been used for this worship by Abraham, such as Mamre and Bethel. Shiloh was in a little valley in the hill-country, safe from the Philistines' attack. The presence of the Ark there made it the central shrine of Israel, and the rallying point for all the tribes. Eli was the hereditary priest there. Recent excavations show that the sanctuary was destroyed about 1050 BC; this was the shock threatened by the Lord to Samuel.

Below
A clay animal, possibly a child's toy.

Samuel was taken serve Eli the high priest when he was very young. At nig he slept in front of the Ark.

THE PHILISTINES CAPTURE THE ARK

The Philistines invaded Israel, and defeated the Israelites, killing about 4000 of them. "Why did the Lord let us lose today?" the Israelite commanders wondered. "Let's bring the Ark from Shiloh, so that the Lord will go into battle with us." So they sent for the Ark and the sons of Eli brought it to the camp.

When the Israelite army saw it, the soldiers gave a shout so great that the earth shook. At first the Philistines were scared, saying, "We're lost! Who can save us from these gods, who destroyed Egypt with every kind of plague." Then, however, they said to each other, "We must be brave and fight as never before, or we'll end up as slaves of the Israelites!" So the Philistines fought hard and slaughtered the Israelites, killing 30,000 foot-soldiers, and capturing the Ark.

One man, from the tribe of Benjamin, took the news back to Shiloh. He had torn his clothes and sprinkled soil on his head, as if someone had died. He found Eli sitting by the roadside, waiting anxiously for news of the Ark. He told Eli that the Israelite soldiers had fled in panic, that his sons were dead and that the Ark had been captured. When Eli heard about the Ark, he fell backwards off his seat. Because he was so old, the fall broke his neck and he died. He had been Israel's leader for forty years.

The Philistines took the Ark to the city of Ashdod, but they suffered so many disasters that they soon hitched up a cart and took it back to the land of Israel.

from 1 Samuel, chapters 4–6

The Ark was captured by the Philistines and taken to Ashdod.

Below
The Ark contained the Law given to Moses by God. It was the symbol of his presence among his people.

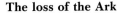

The loss of the Ark
The Ark had been the symbol of God's presence among his people since Moses had been their leader through the desert. It was a wooden chest, plated with gold inside and out, one metre long, by seventy centimetres high and wide.

On top of it were two golden winged creatures, facing each other. Inside lay the two stone tablets of the Law, in memory of the meeting of Moses with God on Mount Sinai, when Moses received the Law. On this occasion, the Israelites carried the Ark into battle as if it were a piece of magic, in hopes that they could force God into winning the battle for them as he had done in the past. So to lose the Ark was an utter disaster. It was the sign that God was no longer with Israel as they had deserted him by being unfaithful to his Law.

So he deserted them until they should repent and return to him. This was the lowest point in Israel's history since the nation began. No worse disaster would befall them until the destruction of Jerusalem by the Babylonians in 587 BC.

However, being in possession of the Ark made the Philistines uncomfortable; being the sign of God's presence, it was no ordinary booty. The Philistines' god was called Dagon, and was probably considered responsible for the fertility of the soil (in Hebrew *dagan* means "grain"). The Philistines offered the Ark in the Temple of Dagon, to show that it was Dagon's spoil. But first Dagon's statue fell over, and when it was put upright again, it fell over and smashed. Then the people of the city were afflicted by the unpleasant and humiliating disease of tumors. So, in spite of their victory in war, the Philistines had to admit that the Lord was more powerful than their god.

Samuel took a jar of olive oil and poured it on Saul's head.

Samuel became the "judge" of Israel. He toured the land settling disputes. When he retired the leaders of Israel went to him and said, "You are old and your sons are not following your example. Give us a king to judge us, like every other nation."

A man called Kish (from the tribe of Benjamin) had a son named Saul. When Kish lost some donkeys, he sent Saul and a servant out to look for them. At that time, if people wanted help, they would say, "Let's go to the seer."

Saul and the servant decided to go to Samuel, the seer, to see if he could tell them where the donkeys were. As they went through the gates of the city they saw Samuel. Samuel had been told by the Lord that Saul would become king.

So he said, "The donkeys you lost have been found. It is you whom all Israel has been seeking!"

Saul answered, "I am from the least important family in the smallest tribe of Israel!" Samuel, however, took Saul home.

At dawn, Samuel said to Saul, "Get up! I shall send you on your way." They walked down the street to the edge of the town. Samuel took a small jar of olive oil and poured it on to Saul's head. Then he kissed him on the cheek and said, "The Lord has chosen you to be the leader of Israel, to govern his people and to save them from their enemies."

from 1 Samuel, chapters 8–10

Left
Saul was chosen by God to be the first king of the Israelites.

Kingship in Israel

To allow a king in Israel was a difficult decision for Samuel. The whole point about Israel was that it was different from other nations. The Lord was their king and ruler; they had made a contract and the Lord alone was head of their nation. His rule was fair and truly in the interests of all the individuals. Samuel warned the elders about the evils of kingship, how kings would exploit their subjects, tax them and make them their slaves – all of which was to happen in Israel soon enough.

The military situation, however, was desperate. The Philistines invaded ever further. Instead of a temporary ruler, a powerful leader was needed, who would protect and defend Israel. Saul was primarily a stable military leader. He remained in his little town in the territory of Benjamin. He did not build a palace or develop a royal court, unlike his successors. He was more like a chieftain than a king.

When Samuel poured olive oil on Saul's head, this was to make him a special person, set apart for God's task. After this, all kings were anointed with oil in this way. Priests were anointed too, and possibly some prophets.

The Lord's choice

Saul was chosen even though his family was the least important in the smallest tribe of Israel (Benjamin). The next king too, David, will be the youngest son, too young to be noticed at all. Throughout the history of Israel runs the theme that God's choice is his own, and is not dependent on human qualities. The younger brother is often chosen in preference to the elder: Abel instead of Cain, Jacob instead of Esau – just as Israel itself was the weakest of all nations when God chose to rescue it from Egypt.

Below
Cosmetic bottles used for storing oils and lotions.

DAVID AND GOLIATH

The Philistines invaded Israel again. The Philistines, however, had a champion, a man named Goliath of Gath. He was nearly 3 metres tall. He wore a bronze helmet, bronze leg-armor and a coat of mail that weighed 55 kilograms. The iron point of his spear weighed over 6 kilograms. Goliath came out and shouted to the Israelites. "I defy the army of Israel. Send a man out and let us fight together!" Saul and his soldiers were terrified. Every morning and every evening for forty days, Goliath came out and made his challenge.

David was the youngest son of Jesse of Bethlehem. He normally looked after his father's sheep, but occasionally went to take food to his brothers, in Saul's army. When he heard about Goliath, he offered to fight him. Taking his staff, he chose five smooth pebbles from the stream and put them into his shepherd's pouch.

When he saw him, Goliath sneered, "Why are you bringing a stick to me – am I a dog? I will feed you to the birds and the beasts." David, however, said, "You fight with sword, spear and javelin; but I fight in the name of the Lord." Running towards Goliath, he took a stone from his pouch and hurled it from his sling. It sank deep into Goliath's forehead and he fell face down on to the ground. David ran over, and used Goliath's own sword to cut off his head. When the Philistines saw that their champion was dead, they fled.

from 1 Samuel, chapter 17, verses 1–51

Goliath, the massive champion of the Philistines, fought David.

Above
A simple sling made from a small piece of leather. A swinging throw releases a stone and gives it speed and direction.

Slings in war
David no doubt learned his skill as a slinger when defending his father's flocks against wild beasts. The sling was also a regular weapon in war. It consisted of a little leather pocket attached to two strings. Normally the slinger fitted a polished sling-stone into this (many specially shaped stones have been found in ancient cities, but David had to collect his own round stones from the river-bed), whirled the sling round his head for speed, and then shot out the stone by releasing one of the strings. The Assyrians were proud of the accuracy of the slingers in their army. In later times Syrians and Egyptians were considered the best slingers in the Greek and Roman armies.

Size and strength
The Philistines seem to have had several gigantic warriors. The Bible mentions four sons of Rapha who fought against Israel. One of them "was a man of huge stature, with six fingers on each hand and six toes on each foot". The Philistines' greatest assets were their iron-tipped weapons which would pierce the softer bronze armor of the Israelites.

The single combat which Goliath suggests was a way of avoiding mass bloodshed. Each side would abide by the outcome of the two champions. The Israelites won this encounter with the Philistines. But there were several more campaigns between Israel and the Philistines. One of the reasons why Saul became jealous of David was his success in battle against them. When Saul gave his daughter to David in marriage he demanded as a bride-price 100 foreskins of the Philistines, for which David would need to kill the Philistines first. As an act of bravado, David provided 200 instead.

David joined King Saul and became a successful soldier. Saul made David commander-in-chief and allowed him to marry his daughter. However, Saul became jealous of David's success and tried to kill him. David fled into the desert with a few followers. He was now an outlaw, hated by the king.

Right
David cuts off the grainer of Saul's cloak.

Saul gathered 3000 men and went looking for David. On the way Saul needed to relieve himself, so he went into a cave near the road.

By chance, David and his men were hiding at the back of that very cave. David crept forward and secretly cut a small piece of cloth from the bottom of Saul's robe. Then, however, he regretted what he had done. "The Lord forbade that I should attack my king, the one the Lord has anointed!" he explained to his men.

Saul got up and left the cave. As he was setting off, David went out and called after him, "My lord king!" Then he bowed his face to the ground and did homage, saying, "Look, my father, at this piece of your robe that I am holding. Why do you listen when people say I plan to harm you? I could have killed you, but I did not. You must realize that I am not plotting rebellion against you. May the Lord judge between us; I will not harm you in any way. I am not worth a dead dog, a flea! Why are you wasting your time chasing me?"

So, for a time, Saul and David were reconciled.

from 1 Samuel, chapter 24

David's hideout at Engedi

Engedi is an oasis beside the Dead Sea. Amid the sandy rocks and cliffs of the surrounding country a plentiful stream comes down in waterfalls. The wild goats and hyrax gather there to drink. It was a good place for David to hide, because it was cut off from Saul's territory by the desert, and there is water to drink and caves for shelter.

The king rejected

Samuel told Saul to muster the army and wait for him to come and offer the sacrifice for them. Samuel was late and Saul offered the sacrifice himself. Samuel told him that he had been rejected by the Lord, and Saul became subject to fits of depression. At the same time David was becoming more popular.

Rivals

As time moved on, Saul grew increasingly fearful of David. He was obviously a more respected fighter than Saul – even the women of Israel knew that and composed a song about it: "Saul has slain his thousands, and David his tens of thousands."

For his part, the Scriptures portray David as refusing to seize the power of the throne. In this passage, David is clearly shown as being prepared to wait until the king died in battle rather than usurping the position to which he had been anointed by the prophet Samuel.

THE ARK IS BROUGHT TO JERUSALEM

Saul died and David became king. He defeated the Philistines and captured the city of Jerusalem, which became his capital.

David took 30,000 hand-picked men to fetch the Ark to Jerusalem. King David and all the Israelites were rejoicing and singing.

He wore nothing but a priest's linen cloth and danced wildly to honor the Lord; in this way the Ark was brought home to shouts of joy and the sound of the shofar horn. David's wife Michal (Saul's daughter), however, was watching from the window. When she saw David leaping and dancing in honor of the Lord, she was filled with contempt for him.

The Ark was taken to the tent of meeting that David had prepared for it, and David offered sacrifices there. Then he went home to his family. Michal, however, sneered at him: "The king of Israel looked really glorious today – dancing in the street before his servants' maids like a common fool!" David replied, "I was dancing for the Lord, who preferred me to your father. I am happy to look a fool for the Lord." And Michal never did have any children.

from 2 Samuel, chapter 6

Above
Baskets and measures of grain in the market.

Jerusalem

David's master-stroke was to capture the ancient fortress of Jerusalem. It lay between the northern territory of Benjamin (where Saul had ruled) and the southern territory of Judah (where David had built up his own power-base). So it was the hinge which joined the two halves of Israel. It was David's own city, won by his private army, captured by a brave stratagem which involved the commander-in-chief squeezing his way up a hidden water-channel.

Then David went one further: he made it the religious capital of the nation by installing there the Ark, the symbol of God's presence among his people. From then on, Jerusalem was the Holy City, the centre of worship of the Lord, and the centre of all the hopes of Israel.

Above
Michal, David's wife.

David the dancer

The linen cloth of a priest, worn by David in honor of the sacred Ark, was too skimpy for Michal's sense of royal dignity. Michal's disapproval was the last straw in her relationship with David. David had married her not out of love but in order to gain the position of son-in-law to King Saul, and Michal risked her father's anger by defending David. When David was expelled from Saul's court, she was given in marriage to another husband. Later, David demanded her back – he could not risk her producing grandchildren to Saul, who might rival him – and her husband followed her weeping as far as he was allowed. But there was no real reconciliation between herself and David, and she died childless.

David has earlier shown his skill as a musician, playing to soothe King Saul in his moods of black depression. He is also given the credit for composing the Psalms of David, those prayers used in the Temple, and still sung in many Christian churches.

Overleaf
As the Ark came into the city of Jerusalem David danced before it. Michal, his wife, looked out of the window.

David's son Absalom gave himself an escort of fifty men. He encouraged people to criticize the king and stole their love by refusing to let anyone pay homage to his father. Finally, he rebelled and David had to flee for his life. David gathered his supporters, and the two armies faced each other. David commanded his generals, "For my sake, don't harm Absalom."

The battle was fought in the forest of Ephraim, and David's troops defeated the rebels. Fleeing from David's men on a mule, Absalom rode under a tree. His head got jammed in the thick branches, but the mule went on, leaving him hanging in mid air. The soldiers reported this to Joab. Joab took three spears and thrust them into Absalom's chest, whilst he was still breathing. Then ten of his men closed in and beat Absalom to death.

David was heartbroken. When David's soldiers heard that he was weeping for his son, the joy of victory turned to sadness. They crept back into the city like deserters. David had covered his face and was wailing loudly, "O my son Absalom, O Absalom, my son, my son!" Joab, however, went to David and said, "You are humiliating your supporters, who today saved the lives of you and your family. You seem to love those who hate you, and hate those who love you. If you stay in here wailing, I promise you that not a man will still be here tomorrow." So David got up and went to sit by the city gates, and greeted the warriors as they returned.

from 2 Samuel, chapters 15, 18–19

Absalom, while fleeing rode under a tree. His head became wedged in the branches and he was left hanging helplessly. Joab killed him.

David the ideal king

The prophet Nathan promised David in God's name that his heirs would reign for ever. From then on the Jews regarded him as the ideal king, the model of kingship. When the last King of Jerusalem was dethroned in 586 BC they began to look forward to a second David, who would refound the kingship as God's representative, the "Messiah" or God's anointed king. Christians accept Jesus as God's king, sent to re-found his kingship over the whole world.

David's family

King David did not manage his family affairs well. First his eldest son, Amnon, raped his half-sister Tamar, and received no punishment at all. Then Absalom, Tamar's full brother, murdered Amnon in revenge; but he was sent into exile for a period of three years. David then allowed him back, but made no attempt to control him. So Absalom stirred up opposition unchecked, though David must have known about his retinue of fifty men. When Absalom finally revolted, David handed Jerusalem over to him without a blow. He was saved only by the loyalty and courage of some of his supporters who stayed behind in the city to work as double-agents for him.

Joab, the commander-in-chief

Joab, David's commander, was a fearsome warrior. There are many stories in the Bible about his pitiless prowess. He was not afraid of disobeying David's orders, as on this occasion, when he had been ordered to spare Absalom. He was quite unscrupulous, and even David seems to have been afraid to rebuke him. One asset he had was that he was left-handed: this meant that he carried his sword on his right thigh rather than his left. On two occasions he cunningly made use of this to kill an opponent who thought that he had come unarmed to a parley. It is not surprising, with this uncompromising toughness, that Joab found David's sorrow at the death of his rebellious son feeble and self-indulgent.

When David died, his son Solomon succeeded him as king. The Lord appeared to Solomon in a dream and offered him anything he wanted. Solomon asked for an understanding mind to rule wisely.

Two mothers brought their case before the king for judgement. One said, "My lord, this woman and I live in the same house. I gave birth to a baby boy and, two days later, so did she. Soon afterwards, in bed one night, she rolled over on to her baby and killed him. So she took my son from me as I slept and put the dead baby in my bed. When I woke next morning to feed my baby, I saw that the child was dead – and that it wasn't my baby but hers." The other woman, however, said, "No! The living child is mine, and the dead child is yours." So they argued before the king.

King Solomon sent for a sword. "Cut the baby in two, so each woman can have half of it," he said. At that, the real mother of the child, who loved him very much, said, "O my lord, don't kill the child. Give him to her!" The other woman, however, said, "Neither of us shall have it. Cut it in two!" Then King Solomon gave his decision: "Give the child to the first woman; there is no need to kill it. She is the mother."

The Israelites realized that Solomon had the wisdom of God.

from 1 Kings, chapter 3, verses 5–28

Right
King Solomon sent for a sword and ordered the baby to be cut in two so that each mother might have half of it.

Infant mortality

In the ancient world the death of children was far more common than it is today. There was little scientific knowledge of the causes of disease until Greek medical science began to develop around 400 BC. In Israel long life was simply regarded as a blessing from God.

Solomon's wisdom

Wisdom was more valued in the Near East than wealth or any other form of authority. It was a very wide term, including fair judgment, but also good manners and sensible behavior. Like the codes of law, Israel shared with its neighboring countries a large body of proverbs and wise sayings, but only in Israel was it recognized that all wisdom comes from the Lord, and cannot be acquired by merely human means. The Israelites reverenced wise men and women because they felt that they shared in God's own wisdom.

Solomon was the king who really organized the court and its ceremonials at Jerusalem, which appear close to those practiced in Egypt. The pharaoh was his father-in-law, and the secretary to his court had an Egyptian name. He also, incidentally, put it on a sound financial basis, creating a system of taxes and labor-contributions which would support quite a large establishment. He gained the reputation for collecting proverbs and wise sayings and several books of these in the Scriptures are attributed to him. His knowledge of natural science was recognized as exceptional; "he could discourse on plants, animals, birds, reptiles and fish."

The earliest collections of proverbs in the Bible may well go back to the time of his reign; these include such sayings as the following.

Proverbs for Life

Bread is sweet when it is got
    by fraud,
    but later the mouth is full of
    grit.

Watch the ant, you lazybones! How hard she works to get her food! When will you wake up? A little sleep, a little slumber, a little folding of the arms to rest – and poverty will come upon you like a robber, and hunger like an armed man.

The fear of the Lord is the beginning of wisdom.

Hatred stirs up trouble,
    but love forgives all wrong.

Fools always think they're right,
but a wise person listens to advice.

Better a dinner of vegetables where there is love than a feast with people who hate you.

Better to be poor and good
    than to have wealth and be a cheat.

A friend loves you all the time,
and a brother sticks with you
through bad times.

Wine is a mocker, alcohol is a fighter;
    whoever is led astray by them is a fool.

It is better to live in the desert
than with an argumentative
and nagging woman.

Meddling in someone else's quarrel
is like grabbing a passing dog by the ears.
from the Book of Proverbs

The wisdom writings
Once Solomon had made a collection of wise

Right
A baked clay chariot found in Syria. King Solomon was said to have 40,000 stalls for chariot horses.

sayings like this; others, for instance King Hezekiah, followed his example. Solomon's are mostly two-line sayings, one line contrasting with the other. Later sayings are often longer. One favorite form of saying is the numerical proverb; in these it is the last line which counts:

There are three things of stately
    tread
    four, indeed of stately walk:
        the lion, bravest of beasts;
        he fears nothing,
    a rooster, a billy-goat,
    and a king when he speaks to
        his people.

Another book attributed to Solomon is a booklet called Ecclesiastes. The author asked many questions about the meaning of life. At times he seems almost to despair: "Futile," he says, "Everything in life is futile." At other times he is more hopeful, as this passage shows:

The seasons of life
There is a right time for everything:
    A time to be born, and a time to die,
    a time to plant, and a time to uproot,
    a time to kill, and a time to heal,
    a time to destroy, and a time to build up,
    a time to cry, and a time to laugh,
    a time to grieve, and a time to dance,
    a time to find, and a time to lose,
    a time to keep, and a time to give,
    a time to tear, and a time to sew,
    a time to be quiet, and a time to talk,
    a time to love, and a time to hate,
    a time for war, and a time for peace.
God has made everything beautiful in its own time, and he has given us the hope of eternity. God's work lasts for ever. Nothing can be added to it, or taken away from it; this is so that we will fear God.

from Ecclesiastes, chapter 3, verses 1–14

THE TEMPLE BUILT BY SOLOMON

In the second year of his reign, Solomon started to build a Temple for the Lord. It was 27 metres long, 9 metres wide and 13 metres high. It also had an entrance room 4 metres wide. All the stone was prepared at the quarry, so that the Temple would be constructed without the noise of hammers, chisels or any iron tool. When he saw that Solomon had started the building, the Lord promised, "If you obey my Laws, then I will keep all the promises which I made to your father David. I will live here among the children of Israel, and I will never leave them."

Solomon finished the Temple. He called together the leaders of all the tribes of Israel. The priests came, bringing with them the Ark, the tent of meeting and all the equipment used in the worship of the Lord. Solomon and the whole nation of Israel gathered and sacrificed so many sheep and oxen that it was impossible to count them. Then the priests carried the Ark into the innermost room in the Temple. They placed it beneath the wings of two huge cherubim. The poles which carried the Ark were so long that they did not fit into the room, but poked out through the entrance. They are still like that to this day. There was nothing in the Ark except the two stone tablets put in by Moses on Mount Sinai.

As the priests left the Holy Place, a dazzling cloud filled the Temple; they had to leave, because the glory of the Lord filled the building. Then Solomon prayed,

> The Lord, you have chosen to live
> in the deepest darkness,
> but I have built you a great Temple
> that you can live in for ever!

from 1 Kings, chapters 6 and 8

Solomon's Temple

The center of Israelite worship had been the Ark, which was housed in the Tent of Meeting. There Israel considered the presence of the Lord to be, and there they went to meet him. After the capture of Jerusalem, King David had built himself a palace, and felt that God deserved a palace too. He bought the land for it, but the actual building was left to Solomon. This was the very first Temple for the Lord, and Solomon made it a building magnificent beyond compare. The shape resembled that of a Canaanite temple. In front there was a bronze "sea", a huge pool resting on twelve carved oxen. The innermost room, where the Ark reposed, was panelled in cedarwood with gold inlay, and the Ark was "sheltered" by two huge winged creatures, whose wings touched in the middle of the room, carved in cedarwood and overlaid with gold. Solomon spared no expense to give glory to his God; the Temple took twenty-two years to build.

Worship in the Temple

The great annual festivals were held in the Temple and it soon became a center of pilgrimage. The Israelites would also go to offer sacrifices when they felt they had displeased the Lord, or in gratitude, or simply to rejoice in his presence. They also offered there the first fruits of their harvest and of their flocks, in recognition that all life and increase was a blessing from him. The Temple had a vast staff of priests, singers, instrumentalists, gate-keepers and treasurers.

The inner room of all was considered to be the exact place where God dwelt. Only the high priest might enter it once a year to offer a special sacrifice for all the people.

In the inner sanctuary of the Temple there were two cherubim carved from olive wood.

THE QUEEN OF SHEBA

When the Queen of Sheba heard about the fame of Solomon, and the Lord his God, she travelled to Jerusalem to test him with some difficult questions. She shared all her problems with Solomon; yet his great insight enabled him to answer and explain everything she asked. When the Queen of Sheba saw how clever he was, and when she saw his palace, his banquets, his civil service, all his servants in their uniforms, his cupbearers and the many burnt offerings he sacrificed in the Temple, well – it took her breath away!

She said to the king, "Everything I heard about you back home is true. Your wealth and wisdom are greater than anything I was told. Praise the Lord your God; he must love the people of Israel very much to give them you as their king, to uphold justice and the Law."

She gave Solomon many tons of gold, along with huge amounts of spices and jewels (more than he had ever been given before). In return, he gave her everything she wanted. Then she and her attendants went back to Sheba.

from 1 Kings, chapter 10, verses 1–13

The Queen of Sheba came to visit King Solomon of Jerusalem.

Left and below
A necklace discovered with other jewellery, pieces of ivory inlay and handles from small boxes.

Solomon's wealth and empire

Solomon became king when the great powers of the Near East were in decline. His father David's influence had reached Damascus and beyond the River Jordan. Solomon's own importance is shown by his marriage to the daughter of the pharaoh of Egypt. Pharaoh would not make a marriage alliance with any unimportant ruler.

Solomon is perhaps the first individual trade-monarch in history. His kingdom was well placed for trade. He served as a middleman between Turkey and Egypt, buying horses in Turkey to sell to Egypt, and chariots in Egypt to sell to Turkey. Solomon also made great advances in warfare. The Israelites had never used chariots. If David captured chariots he burnt them and maimed the horses by hamstringing them. The Scriptures say that Solomon had 1400 chariots and 12,000 horsemen. He built several towns to stable them. The fortifications of these cities are still visible; especially impressive are the massive gateways, with a whole series of rooms for trapping attackers. In addition, he had a fleet which imported gold, silver, ivory, apes and baboons. He also developed the iron-mines at Timnah near the Red Sea port of Elath.

The splendid visit of the Queen of Sheba was probably a trade-embassy. Sheba is in Saudi Arabia, but there were also queens in the north of Arabia at this time. For trade to the West such a queen would be anxious to reach agreement with her western neighbor for the transit of goods through his territories.

Problems of kingship

In spite of Solomon's wisdom, the drawback was that the wealth was not distributed to the people. On the contrary, the great majority of the people had to provide a pool of free labor for his building projects, his expensive army and chariotry, and to finance the expenses of his elaborate court (not to mention his 700 wives). To pay for the craftsmen and cedar provided by King Hiram of Tyre, Solomon gave him twenty villages in the north of the country. All this built up resentment against Solomon, which would break out against his successor.

Below
An ivory cosmetic dish from Egypt.

94

THE DIVIDED KINGDOM

Solomon died, and was succeeded by Rehoboam, his son.

Rehoboam's coronation was at Shechem, and all the tribes of Israel assembled there for the ceremony. When he heard about this, Jeroboam (a rebel who had fled to Egypt during the reign of Solomon) returned. He met the leaders of the northern tribes and they went with him to present their demands to Rehoboam. "Your father made us work hard. We want you to make our life easier, and to lighten the work-load he placed on us. Then we will be your loyal citizens," they said. "Come back in three days," Rehoboam replied.

Rehoboam asked his counsellors for advice. The older men told him to agree; but the young men he had grown up with wanted him to take a hard line with the troublemakers.

Above
The prophet Ahijah took hold of his new cloak and tore it into twelve pieces. Ten of these he gave to Jeroboam.

Three days later the people returned. Rehoboam spoke harshly to them. "My father made you work hard, but I'll make you work harder."

When the Israelites saw that Rehoboam would not listen to them, they cried, "We don't belong to King David's family." They all deserted Rehoboam, and they stoned to death Adoram (who was in charge of the forced labor for the king's building projects). Only the tribes of Judah and Benjamin remained loyal, and Jeroboam became king of the ten northern tribes.

from 1 Kings, chapter 12, verses 1–20

Israel and Judah

During the period of the judges, the twelve tribes were a confederation, not a united kingdom. The great accomplishment of David was to unite the tribes under one king, with one capital, Jerusalem. But Solomon made little attempt to treat the members of the twelve tribes equally. He imposed forced labor on those who lived in the northern half of the kingdom as though they were inferior and mattered less than those in the southern half.

Jeroboam and the northern kingdom

Jeroboam had first attracted Solomon's attention by his energetic work in the forced labor gangs. One day Jeroboam met a prophet called Ahijah. Ahijah suggested revolt to him, by tearing his new cloak into twelve strips, and giving him ten of them: the cloak represented the twelve tribes of Israel, of whom ten would split off with him, and two remain loyal to the king. He fled to Egypt (whose pharaoh was only too happy to foment unrest within his powerful neighboring kingdom) and returned at Solomon's death, ready to act.

Once the north had split off, Jeroboam set about making an independent kingdom. Religious independence was also vital, for his subjects could not pay homage at the Temple in Jerusalem. So he set up his own religious center at the ancient sanctuary in Bethel. But the kings were never so strong or stable in the north as in the south; in the south the same family ruled for another 350 years; they could rely on the Lord's promise to David that his descendants would always keep the throne; in the north one king after another was assassinated, and his whole family killed with him.

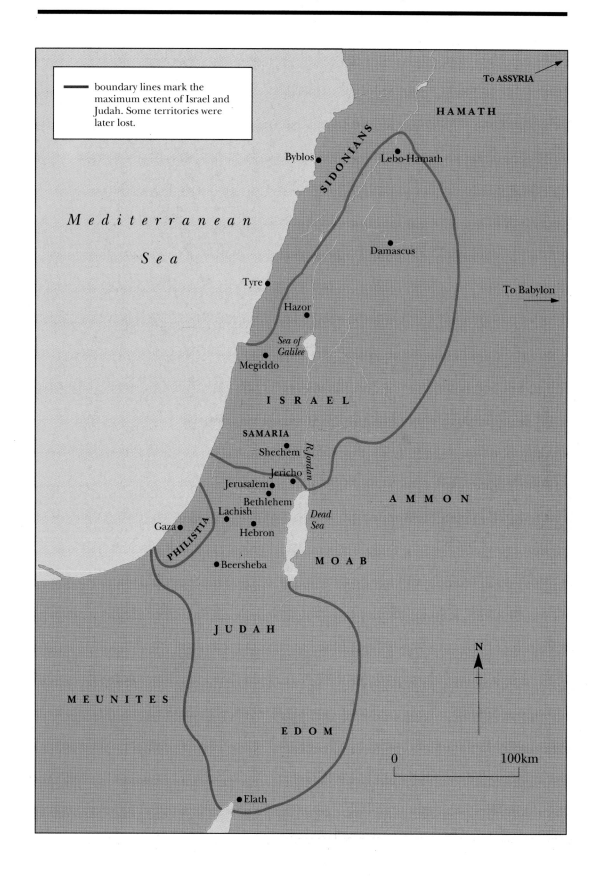

boundary lines mark the maximum extent of Israel and Judah. Some territories were later lost.

To ASSYRIA

HAMATH

Byblos

Lebo-Hamath

SIDONIANS

Mediterranean

Sea

Damascus

Tyre

To Babylon

Hazor

Sea of Galilee

Megiddo

ISRAEL

SAMARIA

Shechem

R. Jordan

Jericho

Jerusalem

Bethlehem

AMMON

Lachish

Gaza

Dead Sea

PHILISTIA

Hebron

Beersheba

MOAB

JUDAH

N

MEUNITES

EDOM

0   100km

Elath

ELIJAH AND THE PRIESTS OF BAAL

Ahab, the seventh king of Israel, angered the Lord more than any king before him. He married a foreigner, Jezebel of Sidon. She introduced the worship of her own god, Baal, and killed the prophets of the Lord. Elijah, the only prophet of the Lord left, proposed a competition between himself and the priests of Baal. He said, "Prepare two bulls for sacrifice. The priests of Baal can pray to their god, and I will pray to the Lord. The god who answers by setting fire to the sacrifice is the true God."

The priests of Baal shouted, and danced round the altar but nothing happened. At noon Elijah started making fun of them. "Pray louder! Maybe he's asleep; you'll have to wake him up." The priests shouted louder and cut themselves with knives and swords until they were bleeding profusely, but there was no reply, no sign and no answer.

Then Elijah built an altar and placed the bull upon it. Three times he soaked the wood with buckets of water. When the time came for the afternoon sacrifice, Elijah prayed, "the Lord, prove now that you are the God of the Israelites." Lightning suddenly came down and burned up everything – sacrifice, wood, altar and all! Then the people fell on their faces and cried, "the Lord is God!" Then Elijah commanded them, "Arrest the priests of Baal," and they killed them all.

from 1 Kings 18, verses 1–40

Jezebel and the priests of Baal

Ahab's father, King Omri, moved the capital of the northern kingdom to Samaria, which is in easy reach of the Mediterranean Sea. He also married his son to the daughter of the priest-king of the flourishing harbor-city of Tyre. Sea-trade, and an opening to the West, were more important to Omri and Ahab than the pure worship of the Lord. Queen Jezebel was a powerful character, and brought along her own worship of Baal and its priests. Just to make sure, she butchered all the prophets of the Lord, except Elijah, who escaped.

Other gods

Baal was a god of storm, rain and lightning (carvings show him carrying a thunderbolt). It was all the more ironical that he could not produce rain for his followers, and that the Lord produced the lightning. Jezebel also encouraged the worship of Asherah, the "wife" of the god Baal, a fertility goddess, whose worship involved sacred prostitution. Whenever men had difficulty over rain and crops, they were tempted to turn for help to Baal, and women, who had difficulty bearing children, to Asherah. Many little statues of both gods have been found in the ruins of the cities of that time. This shows how popular the worship of weather gods such as Baal must have been. But in this account it is the Lord who controls the weather not Baal. The whole competition and sacrifice were a means to end a three-year drought. Baal can do nothing, but the Lord sends lightning and then, just afterwards, sends a wonderful rainstorm.

Elijah soaked the wood three times with water and called on God to set fire to it.

Right
A model of the Canaanite shrine at Hazor dedicated to the moon god.

Jezebel sent word to Elijah that she was going to have him put to death. He was terrified and ran away.

Elijah reached Mount Horeb, and hid in a cave there. He heard the Lord say, "Elijah, what are you doing here?" He answered, "Almighty Lord, I have always served you enthusiastically, but the people of Israel have broken their contract with you, demolished your altars and killed your prophets. I'm the only one left, and they are looking for me, to put me to death."

The Lord said, "Go out and stand before me on the hillside." Then the Lord passed by. A storm of wind swept the mountain, shattering the rocks; but the Lord was not in the storm. An earthquake shook the mountain; but the Lord was not in the earthquake. Then a fire swept the mountain; but the Lord was not in the fire. Then there was a still, small voice. When Elijah heard it, he wrapped his cloak round his head and went out and stood at the cave entrance.

Then the Lord said to him, "Go back to Israel. Anoint Hazael to be King of Syria, and Jehu to be King of Israel. They will destroy all my enemies, and I will save the 7000 people who have remained loyal to me."

from 1 Kings, chapter 19, verses 1–18

Elijah fled from Queen Jezebel's threats and hid in a cave on Mount Horeb. When Elijah heard the still, small voice of God he wrapped his cloak around his head and came and stood at the entrance to the cave.

The voice of the Lord

At the exodus from Egypt, when Israel passed through the desert, the Lord made himself known by storm and earthquake. These were only the prelude to his message. He speaks intimately and quietly to his servants, to those faithful to him. But Elijah still needed to wrap his head in his cloak. This is a sign of reverence and fear; despite his gentleness, the Lord is still an awesome God, and Elijah could not face him directly.

The end of the northern kingdom

Violence and a series of bloody revolutions continued in the northern kingdom for nearly a century. It never did return to serving the Lord faithfully. The prophets had a list of complaints against them: the judges worked only by bribery, the rich oppressed the poor and refused to pay them their wages, they were interested only in drunken revels and in piling up more wealth by exploitation. Their sacrifices disgusted the Lord, because they were not the expression of true religion. The prophets foretold disaster if they did not repent and reform.

The ancient kingdom of Assyria, in the northern part of Mesopotamia, was gathering strength again. The Assyrian armies crossed the River Euphrates and then marched southwards along the Mediterranean coast, conquering one after another of the small states of Syria. Already in 841 BC King Jehu was compelled to pay tribute to the king of Assyria as the price of freedom; he is pictured on a great black obelisk, discovered by a British archaeologist in 1848, bowing to the ground and kissing the feet of the Assyrian, King Salmaneser.

Later Assyrian kings took over a large part of Galilee, then incorporated Damascus into the Assyrian empire. Finally, in 721 BC, the northern kingdom came to an end with the conquest of Samaria. Assyrian policy was to deport the whole population to another part of the empire, thus wiping out all their local loyalties, and leaving them no other loyalty than to the empire itself. The ten northern tribes of Israel were deported, and disappear from history. Their place was taken by a mixed population from elsewhere, who later became known as the Samaritans.

The prophets of Israel typically thundered out their message with, "Thus says the Lord". They were the conscience of the people of Israel, fearlessly scolding kings, priests and people for their failure to live up to the demands of God in the contract made with Moses on Mount Sinai. They also proclaimed that the Lord was a loving God, always ready to forgive. Their sayings were later written down and included in the sacred writings which make up the Scriptures. Here are some of them.

The Cords of Love

When Israel was a child, I loved him;
I led him out of Egypt as my son.
Yet the more I called to him,
the more he turned away from me;
I pulled them towards me
with cords of love.

How can I give you up, Israel?
How can I abandon you?
My heart aches inside me –
I love you too much.
I won't punish you in my anger.
I won't destroy you,
for I am God, not man.
I am the Holy One in your midst,
and I will never destroy you.

from Hosea, chapter 11, verses 1–9

Hosea speaks of family love

Hosea's wife was unfaithful to him, and flirted with other men. But he refused to give her up, and continued to love her passionately. He saw that God's passionate love for the people of Israel was the same. He also saw God's love was like the tender love of a father for his children, taking care of them and desperately hurt when they neglected his love. God loved his people too much to destroy them, however disobedient they were.

Above

Jeremiah buried his loincloth in a cleft in the rocks as God commanded. When he retrieved it later it was ruined as Judah and Jerusalem were to be ruined for disobeying God.

Beware – disaster is coming

Woe to those who are at ease in Jerusalem,
to those who feel safe in the holy places of Samaria.
Woe to those who lie upon beds made of ivory
and stretch themselves on their couches;
who eat lambs and calves
and sing lazy songs to the harp;
who drink wine from bowls
and rub oil on their skin
but don't care that Israel is in ruins.

Listen to this, you who trample on the needy
and destroy the poor.
I saw the Lord beside the altar
and he said, "Smite the pillars
till the building collapses.
No one shall flee away, no one shall escape."

from Amos, chapters 6–9

Amos the shepherd

Amos was a shepherd from a little village in the south. He felt God's message to go to Bethel, the national shrine in the northern kingdom of Israel, and tell the people there that they were rich and corrupt.

A new contract

"Watch!" says the Lord. "The days are coming when I will make a new contract with Israel.

"This is the new contract I will make: I will put my Law within them, and write it in their hearts. I will be their God, and they will be my people. They won't have to say to each other, 'Be the Lord's friend!' Everybody will be my friend – I will forgive their mistakes, and forget their sins."

from Jeremiah, chapter 31, verses 31–34

Josiah was eight years old when he came to the throne.

In the eighteenth year of his reign, he sent his secretary Shaphan to the Temple. "Go to Hilkiah the high priest and give money to the workmen who are repairing the house of the Lord."

The high priest Hilkiah gave Shaphan a book that had been found in the Temple during the repairs. (It was the Book of Deuteronomy, containing the Laws of God.) Hilkiah returned to the palace, and read it out loud to the king.

When Josiah heard what was written in the book, he tore his clothes in horror. "The Lord must be greatly angry with us, because our ancestors have never obeyed his Laws," he told his advisers.

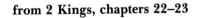

Josiah ordered Hilkiah and the priests to destroy all the equipment used in the worship of Baal and Asherah; they burned them in the fields outside Jerusalem. He dismissed all the pagan priests. In every city Josiah destroyed the pagan shrines which so angered the Lord. He killed the pagan priests, and burned them on their own altars.

Everything else that King Josiah did is recorded in the History of the Kings of Judah.

from 2 Kings, chapters 22–23

Josiah's reforms

Hezekiah's attempts to bring his people back to faithful worship did not last, and his successors energetically brought in foreign forms of pagan worship, even in Jerusalem itself. Half a century later King Josiah made a last, determined effort to improve religious practice, getting rid of the pagan shrines in Jerusalem and on the surrounding hills, and spending lavishly on repairing the Temple.

The Book of Deuteronomy, found during the Temple repairs, is now the fifth book of our Bible. It stresses the same themes as the history of Israel's kings – that obedience to God's Law leads to his blessings whereas disobedience and idolatry result in God's judgment on his people. The book also includes instructions God gave Israel about their way of life because he loved them, and wanted to guide them into happiness. Obedience to these commands was an expression of their love for God in return.

The History of the Kings of Judah

This history is mentioned at the end of almost every reign. Careful records must have been kept, which were later used in compiling the history given in the Scriptures. The Scriptures of course select material from the records, and are chiefly interested in the religious history, always pointing out that faithfulness to the Lord was rewarded with success, and desertion of the Lord with punishment. Josiah, for instance, was rewarded for his efforts by being able to win back much of the territory of the northern kingdom of Israel (helped by a temporary weakness in the Assyrian empire).

THE FALL OF JERUSALEM

Zedekiah was twenty-one years old when he came to the throne, and he reigned in Jerusalem eleven years. Zedekiah disobeyed the Lord like his father Jehoiakim before him. The Lord became so angry that he banished the people of Judah from his presence.

Zedekiah rebelled against King Nebuchadnezzar of Babylon, who invaded Judah. The Babylonians besieged Jerusalem and built siege walls around it. After two years the shortage of food in the city was so severe that the people were starving. Under cover of darkness Zedekiah and his army broke out through the walls, and fled at night towards the Arabah. However, the Babylonian troops chased them. They overtook Zedekiah near Jericho, and scattered his army. They made him watch while they killed his sons. Then they put out his eyes, bound him in chains and led him away to Babylon, where he remained for the rest of his life.

Nebuzaradan, the captain of the king of Babylon's bodyguard, entered Jerusalem. He burned down the Temple and all the houses of Jerusalem, and smashed down the city walls. All the people were taken into exile, except the very poorest, who were left to tend the vineyards and plow the fields. He then looted the Temple, stripping it of its precious contents. Those who had led the resistance were taken to Babylon and put to death.

So was Judah taken into exile from the land.

from 2 Kings, chapter 25, verses 1–21

The sack of Jerusalem

The Babylonians had succeeded the Assyrians as rulers of the Near East.

However, in 601 BC King Nebuchadnezzar was defeated in Egypt, and King Jehoiakim of Judah saw his opportunity to shake off the Babylonian rule. This was a mistake! Nebuchadnezzar besieged Jerusalem briefly in 598 BC, taking into exile in Babylon the king, the military commanders and all the metal-workers (so that there was no one left to make weapons). The Temple and the city were left intact. A sad relic was found in Babylon: the account books for the meals of King Jehoiakim and his family, prisoners at the king of Babylon's table for thirty-seven years.

Nebuchadnezzar installed a puppet-king in Jerusalem, who was to do as he was told. However, unfaithful to the Lord, he was unfaithful to Babylon too, with terrible consequences. The prophet Jeremiah warned Judah's last two kings that their only hope was to be more faithful to the Lord. But Jehoiachim threw his prophecies on the fire. The last king Zedekiah imprisoned Jeremiah in a muddy underground water-tank, where he had only bread to eat. So in 587 BC Jerusalem was sacked and the line of kings from David finally ended.

The siege of Jerusalem

The final sieges of Jerusalem were prolonged by a remarkable engineering achievement: the water supply to Jerusalem could not be cut off. King Hezekiah had a water tunnel 600 metres long cut through the rock, to bring a safe water supply inside the city. It is still possible to walk through this tunnel below Jerusalem.

On the other hand, the siege-engines used by the Babylonians were as advanced as any till gunpowder was invented.

Overleaf
When Jerusalem revolted against Nebuchadnezzar for the second time in 587 BC, the city was sacked.

Below
A Babylonian soldier.

109

BY THE WATERS OF BABYLON

By the waters of Babylon
we sat down and wept,
when we remembered
Jerusalem.

We hung up our lyres,
there on the willow
trees.
For our conquerors told
us to sing for them,
our oppressors
wanted us to rejoice.
They said,
"Sing us one of the
songs of Jerusalem."

But how can we sing to the Lord
in this strange land?

If I ever forget you, O Jerusalem,
may my right hand
shrivel up.
May my tongue never
sing again
if I do not love you,
Jerusalem,
more than my
greatest pleasure!

Left
Date palms.

**from Psalm 137,
verses 1–6**

Babylon

The sack of Jerusalem was a traumatic shock. At first the exiles felt they had nothing left, no country, no king, no Temple, no worship – perhaps even no God. Was their guilt so great that they were no longer the Lord's chosen people? Could they worship the God of Israel in a strange land? They were surrounded by temples of gods, such as Marduk and Ishtar. Babylon was a magnificent city, built on the banks of the River Euphrates. Its grand city-gateway has been taken, brick by brick, to Berlin and re-assembled in a museum there. The broad avenues were decorated with sculptures of dragons and other animals. Its "Hanging Gardens" were one of the Seven Wonders of the Ancient World. The whole city turned out for the great festivals of Marduk and Ishtar. The greatest of these festivals was each spring at the start of their year.

The birth of Judaism

With the guidance and encouragement of the prophet Ezekiel the Jews began to realize that their relationship with the Lord was changed, not ended. They could no longer rely on the Temple or the king, but each individual was offered a personal bond with the Lord – "a new heart", as Ezekiel put it – given by the Lord himself. They needed to keep

themselves separate and distinct from the Babylonians, and so began a new life:

1. Each sabbath (Saturday) they gathered to listen to the holy writings and to pray together in the synagogue; synagogues became the centre of Jewish life everywhere.
2. The traditions of the people, brought and treasured by the exiles, were collected into what eventually became the Hebrew Bible: the stories of the ancestors, more recent histories, the Laws, the sayings of the prophets, and the wisdom literature.
3. The Jewish people took pride in their distinction from the Babylonians. They practised circumcision, upheld special laws about foods, and kept the sabbath day to worship the Lord.
4. They began to emphasize different teachings about the Lord from their earlier history. He was not just their own God, but was God of the whole world. The Lord alone made the world. The Jews developed a contempt for lifeless "idols made with human hands".
5. Through all this, they longed ever more ardently to return to Jerusalem. Jerusalem became in their thoughts a symbol of hope, an ideal city, a city of peace and happiness. One day, the world would be renewed, starting from Jerusalem.

Babylon was the center of a powerful empire.

113

NEHEMIAH INSPECTS THE DAMAGE

Nehemiah was wine-steward to Artaxerxes, the king of Persia. This is his story: The Jews who had been left behind in Palestine and those who had returned there, were in terrible difficulties, and the news from Jerusalem was so bad that I broke down and wept.

The king had never seen me upset before, so he asked me, "Why are you looking so sad? You're not ill; you must be heart-broken." I was very scared, but I said, "May the king live for ever! I can't help it. The city where my ancestors are buried lies in ruins, with its defences destroyed." He said, "What do you want?" I prayed quickly to the God of heaven and asked, "If it please your majesty, if you value my services and will grant my request, I want to go back to Judah to rebuild Jerusalem."

The king allowed me to go. He even gave me a troop of soldiers to accompany me.

I went to Jerusalem. For three days I stared at the devastation, but I did not share my plans with anyone. After I had stayed there three days, I left the city under cover of night with only a few friends and one donkey (on which I rode). I went out and inspected the broken walls. In places, the donkey couldn't get through the rubble.

Then I said to the officials, "You can see the devastation. We must rebuild the walls of Jerusalem." Then I told them how God had helped me with the king. "Let's start building right away!" they replied, and they began to get ready to do the work.

from Nehemiah, chapters 1–2

The return from exile

Fifty years after the sack of Jerusalem, Babylon was conquered by Cyrus, king of the Persians, and founder of a great new Persian empire. This empire was greater than any the world had seen, stretching from the Indian Ocean to the borders of Greece, and including Palestine and Egypt.

Cyrus set about repatriating the subject peoples held captive in Babylon. He even gave back the gold and silver objects from the Temple, which had been stored in the Temples of Babylon, and gave orders that the Temple at Jerusalem should be rebuilt at his own expense. A great procession set off across the desert, and 40,000 people are listed in the Bible as having returned. But many Jews also remained in Babylon; they were already established as bankers and traders, and had no intention of giving up everything to return to an insecure life amid the ruins of Jerusalem.

Life in Jerusalem was insecure and constantly under threat. The land, deserted by the Jews, had been occupied by squatters from the surrounding nations, who resented the return of the Jews as rightful owners. Virtually no progress was made with rebuilding the Temple; only an altar of sacrifice was set up in the ruins. The foundations of the Temple were laid, but then building ceased while legal wrangling took place between the Jews, the squatters and the Persian governors. It was not until twenty years later that the Temple was completed and the first Passover festival celebrated there.

Harassment from the non-Jewish local people continued. Writings from this period in Jerusalem are full of worry, doubt, guilt feelings and disappointment that the glorious return, which they had longed for so eagerly, had turned sour. This state of affairs lasted for another fifty years before Nehemiah made his depressing inspection of the walls in 445 BC.

Nehemiah went out to inspect the broken walls of Jerusalem.

Overleaf
The walls had to be rebuilt and the builders protected by guards from the hostile people who now lived in the land around Jerusalem.

VISIT OF THE WISE MEN

Jesus was born in Bethlehem in Judaea during the reign of King Herod. Soon afterwards, magi arrived in Jerusalem from the East, asking, "Where is the child born to be king of the Jews? We have seen his star in its rising, and we have come to pay homage to him."

When King Herod heard about this he was alarmed, and so was everyone in Jerusalem. He called a meeting of the chief priests and scribes, and asked them where the Christ was to be born. They answered, "The Scriptures say in Bethlehem of Judaea." Herod then held a private meeting with the magi and found out exactly when the star appeared. Then he sent them to Bethlehem, saying, "Look for the child, and inform me as soon as you have found him, so I also may go and pay homage."

Above
Wise men came from the East.

Remarkably, the star rose again in the sky as they set off. They went towards it – it was right over the place where the child was. They were overjoyed. Entering the house, they saw the child and his mother Mary, threw themselves down before him and paid homage to him. Then they opened their caskets and offered him gifts of gold, frankincense and myrrh.

However, they were warned in a dream not to return to Herod, so they went home by a different route. Herod gave orders to kill every male child in Bethlehem under the age of three, but Joseph and Mary had already fled to Egypt.

from Matthew, chapter 2, verses 1–12

The magi

The three kings on Christmas cards were originally only magi, that is, wise men, or sages – the word from which we get "magicians". The spices, frankincense and myrrh are used in spells, so by laying these gifts before Jesus the magicians showed that in his honor they were giving up their false spells and the profits from them (gold).

The gospel also makes a sharp contrast between these foreigners and Herod. Herod and his court were Jews, and should have honored Jesus as the Messiah. But Herod tried to destroy him, and only the foreign wise men did him honor.

Matthew knew this story would remind readers who knew the Bible of the story of Moses as a boy. A king tried to destroy Moses as a baby, but his mother hid him in a floating basket on the River Nile. The king succeeded in killing only other babies. Later Moses fled from his homeland, and returned only when an angel had appeared to say it was safe to go back. Moses was to become the great leader who brought the Israelites out of Egypt and made them a new people. Jesus was the new leader of God's people. He also was saved from being killed by fleeing the country.

History and the massacre of the children

Herod was well known as a bloodthirsty tyrant. He became afraid of being ousted from his throne. So he executed several possible rivals, including his uncle, his wife and even two sons. In a village the size of Bethlehem there would not have been many boys under three. A man like Herod would not have scrupled to kill them all.

The wise men set out.

PRESENTATION IN THE TEMPLE

The child grew up. He became strong and wise. God blessed him. Each year Jesus' parents went to Jerusalem for the festival of the Passover. When he was twelve, they all went together, as Jewish custom required. Although his parents returned to Galilee when the celebrations were over, Jesus – who was now a youth – stayed behind in Jerusalem.

Joseph and his mother did not know about this. They thought he was with some other people, and it was a whole day before they started to look for him among their relatives and friends. When they couldn't find him, they returned to Jerusalem. It was three days before they saw him – in the Temple, attending the public lectures, listening to the Jewish teachers and asking questions. Everybody there was surprised by his intelligence and insight. His parents were shocked. His mother said to him, "Son, why have you treated us like this? Your father and I have been worried sick looking for you." But he said to them, "Why did you look for me? Did you not realize that I must be in my Father's house?"

He returned to Nazareth with them, and obeyed them, but his mother remembered all these events.

from Luke, chapter 2, verses 40–51

Left
On the forehead of this rabbi is a box called a phylactery containing extracts of the Law; he is binding another to his arm to satisfy the command to bind the Law to himself.

The Temple in Jerusalem
The Temple was an amazing building. The outside walls were half a kilometre long, and the largest building-stone was the size of a modern bus. The ten gilded bronze doors were as high as a three-storey house (thirteen metres); a team of twenty men shut them each night. One part of it alone, the Royal Portico, would fit a cathedral with room to spare. It took 18,000 workers fifty years to build.

The Jews regarded Jerusalem as the center of the world, and loved to make the pilgrimage there for the three great feasts of the year. They would come from the different parts of Palestine (a week's walk from Nazareth), from Babylon, from Rome, even from Libya in North Africa. There was a great holiday atmosphere as they came together to sing their national songs and psalms. For they all knew that salvation would come from Jerusalem to the whole world. As well as offerings of grain, wheat and other fruits, there would be a great deal of animal sacrifice, followed by happy feasting.

In the Temple wise people gathered and gave instruction in the Jewish Law. Jesus joined such a group and amazed the older people by the sharpness of his questions.

Jesus the Galilean
Galilee had been converted to the Jewish religion only a century before Jesus' time, and teachers in Jerusalem despised Galileans. They thought they could not even make a proper legal agreement, and Galileans allowed practices which others thought danger-ously immoral, like a man and a woman walking out together at night. People even mocked their accent. Yet in Jesus' time there was a tradition of holy men in Galilee. Some were teachers whose sayings were remembered decades later. Some claimed to work miracles. Their prayers were heartfelt and moving. Jesus will have learnt from such holy men.

Above
This game was played for centuries and is similar to ludo.

Below
Boys playing various games and dice. Game-boards have been found in many places.

The good news about Jesus the Christ, the Son of God, began just as the prophet Isaiah wrote: "I am sending a messenger ahead of you to clear the way, a voice shouting in the desert, 'Make God's road ready, beat a straight path for him.' "

John the baptizer appeared in the desert and called upon the people to be baptized as a sign that they would change their sinful ways. Everybody in Judaea and Jerusalem seemed to be going out to him, to confess their sins and be baptized in the River Jordan. He wore clothes made out of camel's hair, and a leather belt round his waist. He ate locusts and wild honey. "After me comes someone much greater – I am not worthy even to bend down to untie his sandals. I baptize with water, but he will baptize you with the Holy Spirit," he preached.

Jesus came from Nazareth in Galilee and John baptized him in the River Jordan. As Jesus came out of the water he had a vision. He could see into heaven. The Holy Spirit came down on him like a dove, and a voice from heaven said, "You are my Son and I love you; I am pleased with you."

from Mark, chapter 1, verses 1–11

Right
Jesus came from Nazareth of Galilee and was baptized by John.

Jesus baptized by John in the River Jordan.

John the Baptist
The Jews hated the Romans who had occupied their country and made them pay heavy taxes. Many of them reckoned these sufferings were the penalty for their own sins. So they responded eagerly to John's invitation to be sorry for their sins. They hoped that, sometime soon, God would set them free.

The River Jordan
The traditional place where John baptized was where the main road from the East to the Mediterranean Sea crosses the Jordan. The crossing would have been thronged with merchants, soldiers and all kinds of people. John must have cut a striking figure. His dress was deliberately like that of the old Jewish man of God, Elijah, who was expected to come again and lead them to freedom. Dipping in water, or baptism, was a sign of sins being washed away.

The hope of liberation was especially lively in an isolated group at Qumran, on the shore of the Dead Sea, near the Jordan. The library of this group, the "Dead Sea Scrolls", was discovered, hidden in jars in caves, in 1947. They were preparing for the person God would send to free his people, the Messiah. They expected the Messiah to lead them, the Sons of Light, in a great war to annihilate the rest of the world, the Sons of Darkness. John may once have belonged to this group.

The baptism of Jesus
Immediately after the baptism, Jesus had an experience which is described in words first used by the prophets in the Bible. The "heavens torn open" was the sign of God moving into action. The voice he heard spoke words once spoken by the prophet Isaiah. They are the call of God to his special servant, who would lead the Jewish people of Israel back to God. So Jesus realized that the decisive moment had come for his mission to Israel to begin.

Overleaf
Jesus returned from the Jordan and went into the desert.

When Jesus returned from the River Jordan he was full of the Holy Spirit. He felt that the Holy Spirit was telling him to wander about in the desert, so he stayed there for forty days. During this time the Accuser put him to the test.

Whilst he was there Jesus did not eat anything, and he became hungry. It was then that the Accuser said to him, "If you are the Son of God, command this stone to become a loaf of bread." Jesus, however, replied, "The Scriptures say, 'Man shall not live on bread alone.'"

Then the Accuser led Jesus up to a high place and quickly showed him all the kingdoms of the world. He said to Jesus, "You can be ruler over all of them if you will worship me." Jesus answered by saying, "The Scriptures say, 'You shall worship the Lord your God, and serve only him.'"

Then the Accuser brought Jesus to Jerusalem, and set him on a high part of the roof of the Temple, and said to him, "Prove you are God's son – jump! For the Scriptures say, 'God orders his angels to protect you. They will catch you.'" But Jesus answered him. "The Scriptures say, 'Do not put the Lord your God to the test.'"

Below
Jesus in the desert.

When the Accuser had tried every test, he left Jesus alone, waiting for a better opportunity. Jesus returned to Galilee and was praised by everybody.

from Luke, chapter 4, verses 1–15

The Accuser

The traditional picture of Satan (the Devil), dressed in red, with horns, tail and pitchfork, comes from the mystery plays of the Middle Ages. The Jews first thought of Satan as a recording angel, whose job was to write down all the evil deeds done by a person, and present them as an Accuser when that person died and came to be judged. Later, as in this account of Jesus in the desert, it became his job actually to present temptations to people, to test their faithfulness to God. So, for the Jews, the Accuser became the Tempter.

The testing of God's son

After his baptism Jesus needed to prepare for his mission by forty days in the solitude of the desert. In the same way the prophet Elijah spent forty days in the desert preparing for his mission to the King of Israel 900 years before. Jesus must have asked how God wanted him to fulfil his mission. Was it by winning followers through providing them with plenty of good things (turning stones into food)? Was it by driving out the Romans and making a world empire (ruling all the kingdoms of the earth)? Was it by showing his personal power through flashy miracles (throwing himself off the roof of the Temple)? All these were false ways to fulfil his mission.

The testing of Israel

Luke relates this event in the form of a dialogue with the Accuser, in which each quotes Scripture at the other. All these texts come from the story of the Jewish people's wanderings for forty years in the desert, when the Jewish nation was tested too – and often grumbled against God or worshipped false gods. God's people, Israel, failed; but God's son, Jesus, remained faithful.

Jesus began to preach his message, "Change your evil ways, for God's kingdom is coming soon."

As he walked by the Sea of Galilee he saw two brothers – Simon who is called Peter ("Rock") and Andrew his brother. They were throwing a casting-net into the sea, for they were fishermen. Jesus said to them, "Come with me, and I will teach you to bring in people, not fish." Immediately, they left their nets and followed him.

A little further on, he saw another two brothers, James the son of Zebedee, and John his brother, in the boat with their father, mending their nets. Jesus called them, and immediately they left the boat and their father and followed him.

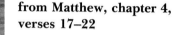

from Matthew, chapter 4, verses 17–22

Left
Fishermen on the Sea of Galilee.

The sea and the fishermen

The Sea of Galilee is only nineteen kilometres long by nine kilometres wide – Luke calls it a "lake" – but is still the home of a thriving fishing industry. These first four who followed Jesus were not penniless, but were running a successful business based at Capernaum, on the north shore of the sea. They had plenty to give up. All the accounts of the call of Jesus' disciples stress that there was no hesitation: their response was immediate and total.

The Christian fish

Fish often come into Jesus' teaching. He used everyday things to enliven his message. He once compared his followers to a catch of fish, some good and some bad; the bad ones must be thrown away. The fish also became a secret sign among the early Christians: in Greek the five letters of "fish" (*i-ch-th-u-s*) also stand for "Jesus Christ, Son of God, Saviour" (**I**esous **Ch**ristos **Th**eou **U**ios **S**oter).

The Twelve

Jesus called twelve followers to be his special disciples and took special care to instruct them. They were a rough crew, often slow to understand, quarrelling among themselves, even rude and sarcastic to Jesus. Eventually one of them sold Jesus to his opponents, and the rest ran away. Yet in choosing twelve of them Jesus was deliberately imitating the pattern of the people of the Jewish nation Israel, a pattern of twelve tribes, and each of the twelve tribes was represented by one of the disciples.

Simon "the Rock"

Simon the fisherman was an impulsive and energetic character, full of affection and good intentions. He promised to follow Jesus through thick and thin, and then denied him three times within a few hours, under no greater pressure than a serving-girl's questions. But he was the first to recognize Jesus as the Messiah, and Jesus made him the leader of the Twelve, giving him the nickname "Rock" (*petros* in Greek means rock).

There is a Christian tradition that he founded the Christian community in Rome, and there, according to tradition, he was martyred, crucified upside-down. Many hold that his tomb can still be seen in the excavations under the Church of St Peter in Rome, near the ancient racecourse where many Christians gave their lives for their faith.

Overleaf
Walking by the Sea of Galilee Jesus called the fishermen who were to become his first disciples.

A WEDDING AT CANA

There was a marriage feast in the village of Cana in Galilee. Mary the mother of Jesus was there, and Jesus and his disciples had also been invited.

Then they ran out of wine. Mary went and told Jesus. Jesus said to her, "Dear lady! What am I to do with you? My hour has not yet come." Mary told the servants, "Do whatever he tells you."

In the room were six stone jars. Each held two or three *metretes* of water, so that people could purify their hands and dishes before eating – as Jewish custom demanded. Jesus told the servants, "Fill the jars with water," and they filled them up to the brim. Then he told them, "Take some out and give it to the master of ceremonies." They did so, and when the master of ceremonies tasted the water that had now become wine, he called the bridegroom and said to him, "Most men give out the best wine first, and leave the poor wine until everybody is too drunk to notice; but you have kept the good wine until now." Nobody but the servants knew where the wine had come from. It was the first sign Jesus gave to reveal God's power at work in him, and his disciples believed in him.

from John, chapter 2, verses 1–11

Below
A bride shows off her wedding dress.

The wedding-feast

The whole village would be invited to a wedding-feast, and it might well last a week. In that time a good deal of wine would be drunk. Hospitality has always been important in the East, and if the wine ran out it would bring great shame on the bridegroom's family.

In a dry country, where every drop of water is precious, fresh water is a vivid sign of life, and the Law, God's gift of himself to the Jews, was thought of as giving life to Israel. So in the Bible, the Jewish Law is often compared to water. But Jesus takes this water and changes it into something even better: wine as the proper celebration of a wedding feast. This was why the disciples saw Jesus' action as a sign of his heavenly glory. But it was still a long time before they all fully understood who Jesus was.

The stone jars

In Judaism ritual purity was very important. God was separate from ordinary life, and it was necessary to wash off the dirt of ordinary life before approaching him. Even by the time of Jesus, Jewish teachers had elaborate rules about purification before meals. But Jesus told his disciples that purity consists in the words and actions which come from a person himself, not in what someone eats and drinks.

The jars were large. A *metretes* was about 40 litres, so Jesus provided an enormous quantity – between 480 and 720 litres (20–30 gallons) – of wine.

THE SERMON ON THE MOUNT

When Jesus saw the huge crowds, he went up to a hilltop. He sat down with his disciples round him. Then he began to speak and taught them, saying.

"Blessed are those who are poor in spirit, for the kingdom of heaven belongs to them.
Blessed are those who mourn, for they will be comforted.
Blessed are the humble, for the earth will belong to them.
Blessed are those who seek to do what is right, for they will be given what they want.
Blessed are those who are merciful, for they will be treated with mercy.
Blessed are the pure in heart, for they will see God.
Blessed are the peacemakers, for they will be called the children of God.
Blessed are those who are treated badly for doing right, for the kingdom of heaven belongs to them.

Blessed are you who are persecuted for my sake, for your reward is great in heaven."

from Matthew, chapter 5, verses 1–12

Right
Flowers above Galilee.

Jesus the Teacher

When Matthew describes Jesus taking his seat on a hilltop for his great teaching, called the Sermon on the Mount, he is comparing Jesus to Moses, who also gave the Law solemnly from a mountain.

In fact Matthew here gathers together into one great collection teachings which Jesus would have given on many different occasions. Jesus travelled around proclaiming the Kingship of God, and he must have repeated his main teachings often, using slightly different words.

In those days, when books were rare and expensive, people were far more used to learning by heart. From their earliest schooling onwards, Jewish children learnt large parts of the Scriptures by heart, and later on also the sayings of the rabbis. Jesus made it easier to remember his teaching by using lively stories about familiar objects. Often he taught not by giving answers, but by asking questions, so that his hearers were challenged to think out the answers and make them their own: "Which is easier to say, 'Your sins are forgiven' or 'Get up, pick up your mat and walk'?" So, having said this, he left his audience to wonder whether he could really forgive sins as well.

Jesus often used a question and answer format followed by a brief saying. "Once, the Pharisees asked the question, 'Should we pay taxes or not?' Jesus replied, 'Whose head is on the coinage?' They answered him, 'Caesar's'. Jesus made his point, teaching, 'Pay Caesar what belongs to Caesar, and God what belongs to God.' "

The early Christians, and the gospel-writers who represented them, were not interested in Jesus merely as a historical figure of the past. They believed he had risen again. They applied his teaching to their own lives and their own circumstances.

Jesus gathered his disciples around him.

144

HEALING A PARALYSED MAN

Jesus had made the town of Capernaum his base. Word got round that he was at home. When Jesus preached, so many came to see him that the house was too small for all the people, who spilled out of the door into the street. When four men came bringing a paralysed man to be healed, therefore, they were unable to get near. So they went up on to the roof and dug a hole through it, and lowered into the room the mattress on which the man was lying. Seeing how much these men trusted him, Jesus said to the paralysed man, "My son, your sins are forgiven."

Some scribes who were there were wondering, "Is this blasphemy? Surely only God can forgive sins." Jesus realized immediately what they were thinking, and said to them, "Why are you disturbed by this? Which is easier to say to this paralysed man, 'Your sins are forgiven', or, 'Get up, pick up your mat and walk'? I will show you that the Son of Man has the authority to forgive sins." So he said to the paralysed man, "Get up, pick up your mat and go home."

Immediately, while everybody watched, the man got up, picked up his mat and left. They were all stunned and praised God, saying, "We have never seen anything like that before!"

from Mark, chapter 2, verses 1–12

The house and the sick man

Capernaum was a little fishing village on the shore of the Sea of Galilee. The normal houses in a Palestinian village at this time consisted of a single room, box-shaped and with a flat roof. This roof could be reached by a staircase and was used for drying fruit or grain, or even for sleeping in summer. It was made of branches laid on wooden beams, with a layer of mud on top. It would have been easy to break through to get into the room below.

The sick man was not necessarily paralysed in the modern sense of the word, that is, unable to move. The Greek word means only that he was bedridden and unable to walk around. Jesus never effects his cures unless people have first shown their trust in him; there must always be a personal commitment to Jesus first. In this case, the sick man never spoke a word. It seems that Jesus looked at the faith of the four bearers who showed their trust in his power and wished for a cure, though the sick man must have put up with an uncomfortable and frightening ride!

For Jesus, his miracles were signs that the prophecies of the renewal of the world were being fulfilled. The prophets of the Old Testament had always looked forward to a time when God would wipe away all evil, sorrow, sickness, suffering and strife, bringing back the peace and harmony of paradise. Jesus saw his cures as part of his Good News that God was to be truly King at last, fulfilling these promises.

> Then the eyes of the blind will be opened,
> The ears of the deaf unsealed,
> Then the lame will leap like a deer,
> And the tongue of the dumb sing for joy.

The authority of Jesus

Several of Jesus' sayings show that he thought of himself as God's special envoy, the Servant of God prophesied in the Jewish Scriptures. Yet the gospels show he himself claimed powers and authority which belong only to God.

He claimed to forgive sin. He claimed authority to make changes in the Law which was given personally by God to Israel. By choosing his twelve disciples he founded his own new people of God to take the place of the twelve tribes of Israel as God's people.

The friends of the paralysed man removed the roof of the room above Jesus so they could let their friend down on his mat.

NICODEMUS FINDS JESUS

One night a Jewish leader named Nicodemus, a Pharisee, came to see Jesus. "Rabbi, we know you are sent by God; no one could do the miracles you do, unless God was with him," he said.

Jesus told him, "No one can see God's kingdom without being born again." Nicodemus said to him, "How can anyone be born again? It isn't possible to go back into the mother's womb for a second time."

Jesus replied, "Amen, amen, I say to you, no one can enter God's kingdom without being born of water and the Spirit. The body gives birth to the physical side of human nature, but the Holy Spirit gives birth to the spiritual side. It is like the wind – it blows wherever it wants. You can hear it, but you don't know where it has come from or where it is going. The Holy Spirit grants new birth to people in just the same way."

"How can this be?" asked Nicodemus. Jesus replied, "Are you a teacher of Israel and yet you don't know these things? As Moses lifted up the snake in the desert, so must the Son of Man be lifted up, so that everyone who believes in him may have eternal life. For God so loved the world that he gave his only-begotten Son, that anyone who believes in him should not perish, but have eternal life."

from John, chapter 3, verses 1–16

Left
A member of the Sanhedrin, the supreme council of the Jews.

Nicodemus the Pharisee visited Jesus by night to keep his meeting secret from other Pharisees.

Nicodemus the Pharisee

The Pharisees were the strictest group of the Jews. For all the Jews the Law was the gift of God to their nation and the sign of God's special love. Obedience to the Law was therefore an expression of love in return, as children obeying their Father. But the Pharisees were the most careful, for they thought that God would really be their King if the Law was perfectly obeyed. They sometimes tied themselves in knots in their anxiety to obey the Law in every detail, and ended up failing to show the love and generosity which the Law commands.

Nicodemus was a teacher of the Jewish Law, and he comes to Jesus as to a great teacher: he calls him "Rabbi", acknowledging him as Master.

The Son of Man

This strange expression seems to have been the way Jesus liked to refer to himself. Literally in Aramaic it means "man" or "human being", but at the time of Jesus it was often used in making a personal claim which might otherwise seem to be a boast (like the English "one" in "one often finds . . ."). So Jesus used it when his claims might shock or distress: *The Son of Man has nowhere to lay his head. The Son of Man has power on earth to forgive sins. The Son of Man will be delivered up to death.* All these seem to be general statements, when in fact Jesus is referring to himself.

But the gospel-writers often see Jesus using this expression to lay claim to the power over the whole world, given to the son of man in the Book of Daniel.

I was gazing into the visions of the night,
When I saw, coming on the clouds of heaven,
As it were a son of man.
He came to the one most venerable.
On him was conferred rule, honor and kingship,
And all peoples, nations and languages became his servants.

149

THE SAMARITAN WOMAN

Jesus came to the town of Sychar in Samaria. Jacob's Spring was there, and Jesus, who was tired after the journey, sat down by the well. It was about noon. A Samaritan woman came to draw water, and Jesus said to her, "Give me a drink." The disciples had gone into town to buy some food.

Jews normally refuse to have anything to do with Samaritans, so the woman said to him, "How is it that you, a Jew, are asking me, a Samaritan woman, for a drink?" Jesus answered, "If you knew the wonderful thing God could give you, and to whom you are speaking, you would be asking me to give you the Living Water."

"Sir, you don't have a bucket, and the well is deep; how could you get any spring-water? Are you greater than our ancestor Jacob, who gave us this well – he drank here, you know, he and his sons and his cattle," said the woman.

"Everyone who drinks this water will eventually become thirsty again," said Jesus, "but whoever drinks the water I give will never thirst again. It will be as though they have a bubbling spring of eternal life inside them." The woman replied, "Sir, give me this water so I shall never thirst again; I won't have to come out here to draw water every day."

"Go call your husband," said Jesus to her. The woman replied, "I have no husband." "Exactly!" said Jesus, "for you have had five husbands, and the man you are living with now is not your husband."

"Sir, I realize now that you are a prophet," said the woman, "but we worship here, and not in Jerusalem." Jesus replied, "Religion is not about where you worship. God wants worshippers who will worship him in Spirit and in Truth." The woman said to him, "The Messiah, the Christ, is coming. When he comes, I know he will explain all this to us." Jesus said, "I, who am talking to you, am he."

At this point the disciples returned. They were amazed he was talking to a woman, but none of them said anything. So the woman left her water-jar and went into the city. "Come and see a man who told me everything I ever did," she told the men, and they all left the city and went to Jesus. Many believed in him, because of what the woman said.

from John, chapter 4, verses 5–30, 39

Jesus and the Samaritan woman.

Above
A Samaritan woman drawing water from the well.

The Samaritan woman

In those days and that country it was most unusual for a man to speak to an unknown woman. From the beginning she was clearly amused by a Jew making a request of her, for Jews and Samaritans were bitter enemies. They had been brought into the country as captives centuries before. They had never fully accepted the Jewish way of life.

Christ – Messiah

Near the end of their conversation, the woman spoke of the Messiah, the Christ. *Christos* is Greek, *messiah* is Hebrew. Both mean "the anointed". Kings and priests were touched or anointed with the sacred oil to show that they were specially linked to God. So Jesus, the greatest of God's messengers, is called "the anointed" to mark his special task from God and the special link with God which enables him to perform it.

CALMING THE STORM

When evening came, Jesus said to the disciples, "Let's sail across to the other side of the sea." So they left the crowds and took him over. A number of other boats followed them.

A great squall of wind blew up, and waves smashed over the boat, so that it began to fill with water. Jesus was in the stern of the boat, asleep on a cushion. They woke him up. "Teacher, don't you care if we die?" they asked.

Jesus stood up and rebuked the wind, and said to the wind and sea, "Be silent! Be still!" The wind died down, and there was a great calm. Then Jesus turned to his disciples and said, "Why are you so scared? Don't you trust in God?"

They were terrified and said to one another, "Who is this, that even the wind and sea obey him?"

from Mark, chapter 4, verses 35–41

Left
The Sea of Galilee.

The sea
The Sea of Galilee lies 200 metres below the level of the Mediterranean Sea, deep in the Jordan Valley. When the wind blows, it funnels down deep clefts in the surrounding hills and can whip the sea into a raging storm within a few minutes.

The power of a huge quantity of water is always awe-inspiring, and fishermen would be especially aware how dangerous it could be. In some ancient stories the sea was a goddess from whom the other gods were born. The heaving and uncontrollable mass of the sea made the Jews think of the frightening chaos from which the world was formed. In their minds God held back this chaos from engulfing the world, and, if he stopped doing this, the universe might at any moment revert to chaos. Control over the seas seemed to be the strongest proof of God's control of natural forces.

This was why the disciples were so stunned at Jesus' calm and effortless control of the sea. They saw him as one who exercised the power which belongs to God.

The disciples and Jesus
The disciples were very eager, and yet they were slow to learn. At first crowds flocked to Jesus. But they eventually faded away and Jesus was left with his little band of quarrelling followers. As in this story, they could be quite sarcastic to him. He often rebuked them for their lack of faith or trust in him. It was a long time before they understood that he was the Messiah. At last they did, and he began to explain that as the Messiah he must suffer. They found this just as hard to understand – and also that as his followers they must suffer and be persecuted too.

Time for understanding
The Gospel of Mark placed much more emphasis on the slowness of the disciples than did the other gospels. In Mark's gospel Jesus carefully chose his time to reveal his nature and the consequences of following him.

Jesus did not have much time to prepare his disciples to carry his message out into the world. We do not know how long his preaching mission lasted. The annual Jewish festival of the Passover is mentioned three times in the gospel, so some people guess that Jesus was teaching for three years. But this is only a guess.

Jesus lay asleep in the stern of the boat. A great windstorm arose, and the waves beat into the boat.

JAIRUS' DAUGHTER

Jesus had just crossed the sea and landed at Capernaum. A great crowd gathered around him.' Jairus, an official of the synagogue came and knelt at Jesus' feet, saying, "My daughter is at the point of death, but if you come and lay your hands on her, she will be made well and live." Jesus went off with him, and the crowd followed. On their way, messengers came from the official's house saying to Jairus, "Your daughter has died; you don't need to bother the Rabbi now." Overhearing them Jesus, however, said to Jairus, "Don't be afraid, trust me."

When they came to the house, and Jesus saw the women wailing and howling, he said, "Why are you making such a fuss? The girl is not dead but asleep." They openly laughed at him, but Jesus pushed them out. Taking the child's father and mother with him he went in, took the girl's hand and said to her, "Get up." She got up and started to walk around. She was twelve years old. They were stunned with amazement, but Jesus ordered them to tell no one what had happened. Then he said, "Give her something to eat."

from Mark, chapter 5, verses 22–24, 35–43

The synagogue

From 606 to 538 BC the Jews were forced to live in Babylon, hundreds of miles from Jerusalem. As they were not able to go to the Temple in Jerusalem they started to build local places of worship called synagogues. The doorway always faced Jerusalem, as a symbol of their longing to return to the Holy City. Services were held on sabbaths (our Saturdays) and festival days. There, in a special chest or "Ark", was kept the sacred scroll of the Law. Synagogues were centres where Jews would gather to discuss the Scriptures and teach the Law. One of the readings from the Scriptures was always from the Jewish Law which they regarded as God's instructions for life. It explained how God's people should respond to his love for them by obeying his commandments.

The synagogues were also centres of hospitality ("A sabbath without a guest is no sabbath", runs a Jewish saying) and always had a place for looking after travellers. As the Jews came to be scattered in communities all over the world, the synagogue became the centres of Jewish life, as they still are today.

The council of elders

The local community (here a fishing village) and the synagogue were governed by a council of elders with an elected president. Jairus was the president of the synagogue at Capernaum. The foundations of Jairus' synagogue can still be seen beside the lake at Capernaum. On the same foundations stand now the ruins of a fine synagogue built a century later.

Death

The death of children was much more common in those days than it is now. Mourning for the dead was basically designed to show the opposite of festivity. So instead of smart, clean clothes and handsome coiffures, people wore dirty, torn clothing and threw ashes on their heads. Instead of joyful songs, there were howls and shrieks. Often professional mourners were hired, and sometimes flute-players too. Such music was thought to be a particularly sad sound.

In earlier centuries the Jews had believed that the dead flitted around in a sort of ghost-world under the earth. By Jesus' time, most of them had come to believe that those who had lived good lives would rise to life again all together at the end of time.

When Jesus came to Jairus' house, he saw the flute-players and the crowd making a commotion.

THE DEATH OF JOHN THE BAPTIST

Herod Antipas, the ruler of Galilee, had arrested John the Baptist, chained him and thrown him into prison. Herod had done this to please his wife Herodias.

Herod had married Herodias even though she had formerly been the wife of his brother Philip. John the Baptist had told Herod that this was wrong: "It is against God's law to marry your brother's wife while he is still alive."

Herodias, therefore, held a grudge against John, but she was not able to order his death because Herod was afraid of him. Knowing him to be a holy man, Herod protected John; he enjoyed hearing his preaching, though it disturbed him.

Herodias got her chance when Herod held a feast on his birthday. All the nobles, military commanders and leading citizens of Galilee were invited. Herodias' daughter came in and danced for them. She pleased them so much that Herod swore he would give her anything she asked for – even half his kingdom.

The girl went out and said to her mother, "What shall I ask for?" Herodias answered, "Ask for the head of John the Baptist." The girl rushed back to Herod and said, "I want the head of John the Baptist on a plate – right now!"

The king was sad, but he could not refuse her because of the promises he had made, and because all the guests were watching.

from Mark, chapter 6, verses 17–26

Above
Food for feasts was provided in large bowls for the diners.

The Dance of Death

We do not know how old the girl was in this story or even her name. Medieval writers thought that her name was Salome (a daughter of Herod mentioned by the Jewish historian Josephus). They portrayed her as an erotic teenage beauty. She could, however, have been quite young. The villain of the story is the scheming Herodias.

John's death is a threat to Jesus. The reason why Mark tells this story is that Herod thought Jesus was a reincarnation of the Baptist whom he had killed. Each began in the desert, each preached repentance and the Kingship of God, each refused to compromise.

The Jewish historian Josephus has a slightly different story, also stressing Herod's respect for the Baptist, but giving the reason for his imprisonment as Herod's fear that he would start a rebellion.

Herod Antipas

He was not really a king, only a tetrarch (from two Greek words, *tetartos* meaning quarter and *arche* meaning rule), ruler of a quarter of the kingdom of his father, Herod the Great. In Luke's account of the Passion of Jesus, Herod was in Jerusalem for the feast, and Pilate tried to shift responsibility for getting rid of Jesus on to him. Afterwards his land was invaded and he was defeated by the father of the wife he had left to marry Herodias. He ended his days in exile.

When Herod's birthday came, the daughter of Herodias danced before the company.

Below
Music and dancing accompanied large important feasts.

156

FEEDING THE FIVE THOUSAND

Right
Five loaves and two little fish.

Just before the Passover festival, Jesus crossed the Sea of Galilee. He was being followed by a huge crowd who had watched him heal the sick. He climbed a hillside and sat down with his disciples. Jesus looked up and saw a great crowd approaching. He said to Philip, "Where can we buy loaves of bread for all these people to eat?"

Philip answered, "We could spend 200 *denarii* on bread, and they would still have only a little each." One disciple, Andrew the brother of Simon Peter, said, "There is a young lad here who has five barley loaves and two little fish, but how could they feed so many?"

"Make the people sit down," said Jesus. The crowd, about 5000 people, sat down on the hillside (which was a large grassy area). Then Jesus took the loaves of bread. When he had given thanks to God, he handed it out among the crowd; he did the same with the little fish. When everybody had eaten as much as they could, he said to the disciples, "Collect all the left-over bits of bread so that we do not waste anything." They gathered twelve baskets full of pieces of bread. The people began to talk among themselves: "He must be the Prophet we are expecting," they said.

The crowd tried to seize Jesus and make him king, but he escaped and went across the lake.

from John, chapter 6, verses 1–15

There was a boy with five loaves and two little fish.

The feast of the Messiah

This is one of the very few scenes in the ministry of Jesus recounted in all four gospels; obviously they considered it especially important. By providing food for his followers in the countryside, Jesus was doing what other great figures in Jewish history had done. In the desert after the escape from Egypt, Moses had provided bread in the form of manna. The prophet Elisha miraculously provided bread for his followers when they were tired (but he fed 100 people from 20 loaves; Jesus' miracle was 20 times as great). The onlookers realized that Jesus was like these great leaders of the past. They tried to make Jesus king, in the hope that he would lead a revolution against the Romans. He was not a revolutionary leader and he avoided this.

The crowd of 5000 was only an approximate figure. Two hundred *denarii* would provide lots of bread; a *denarius* was a day's wage for a farm-hand, but even 200 denarii would not have provided sufficient food. All were filled and twelve baskets of scraps were left over.

Was this a "miracle of generosity"? Did the boy share his parcel of food and thus inspire all the others to bring out the little parcels of food they had with them, so that everyone had enough? This explanation misses the point. Those familiar with the Old Testament and the first Christians realized that the gospel-writer was showing that Jesus was greater than the great prophets and that John specifically saw it as a sign that Jesus was the Messiah who miraculously provided a banquet for his followers.

Above
Baskets of scraps gathered up so that nothing was wasted.

Immediately after feeding the five thousand, Jesus made the disciples get into a boat, to go ahead of him to the other side of the Sea of Galilee, while he dismissed the crowds.

Then he went alone into the mountains to pray, and stayed there by himself late into the night. By this time the disciples were well out into the middle of the sea, and the boat was being tossed about by the waves, for there was a strong wind against them.

Just before dawn, Jesus came towards them, walking on the sea. When the disciples saw him they were terrified. "It is a ghost," they said, and they shouted aloud with fear. Immediately Jesus spoke to them, saying, "Be bold! It is me! Don't be afraid."

Peter answered Jesus, "Lord, if it really is you, tell me to come to you on the water." So Jesus said, "Come here." Peter got out of the boat, and started walking on the water towards Jesus. But when he saw the strength of the wind, he was afraid and started to sink. "Lord, save me!" he cried.

Jesus immediately reached out his hand and grabbed him. "You still do not trust me," he said. They got into the boat, and the wind died down. Then everybody in the boat worshipped Jesus. "Truly you are the Son of God!" they said.

After they had crossed over, they came to land at Gennesaret. When the people there recognized him, they sent messengers throughout the region and brought all who were sick to him. They begged him to let them touch even the fringe of his cloak; and all who touched it were healed.

from Matthew, chapter 14, verses 22–36

A story of faith?

The disciples could not believe their eyes. Walking on water was just as remarkable for them as it would be for us today. In the Book of Job they would have read about God:

> Who alone spreads out the heavens
> and treads on the waves of the sea.

They would have been reminded of this as they saw Jesus walking on the water. So the disciples thought they were in the presence of the divine. This was the first time any of the disciples hailed Jesus as Son of God.

Those who seek to "explain" miracles suggest that Jesus was in fact walking on a sandbank, or in the shallow water. But would fishermen have been surprised at this?

Peter's daring

Peter responded to Jesus' assurances by boldly walking toward Jesus on the water. But it proves to be another example of Peter's enthusiasm followed by speedy collapse in the face of difficulties! The early Church recognized a symbolism in Matthew's description of events; in Peter's setting out bravely on his own, then sinking, and surviving only because he cried out, "Lord, save me." For later Christians the ship represented the Christian community, tossed up and down on a sea of difficulties. Left to themselves, Christians would drown but they took great comfort that they could survive only with Jesus' help.

Early in the morning Jesus came towards them walking on the water.

160

THE TRANSFIGURATION OF JESUS

Jesus and his disciples were visiting the villages near Caesarea Philippi. As they travelled, he asked them, "What are people saying about me?" They told him, "Some say that you are John the Baptist; some, Elijah; and others, one of the prophets." "And who do you say I am?" he asked them. Peter answered, "You are the Messiah." Jesus strictly ordered them not to tell this to anyone.

He told them that the Son of Man would suffer terrible things, be rejected by the Jewish leaders and be executed, but that he would rise again after three days. He spoke so bluntly that Peter took him to one side and told him to stop. Jesus, however, turned his back on Peter and rebuked him: "Get behind me, Tempter. You are looking at this from a human point of view, not from God's." He called over the crowd and the other disciples. "If anyone wants to be my follower, he must deny himself, take up his cross and follow me."

Six days later, Jesus took Peter, James and John up a high mountain, where, in front of their eyes, he was transformed. His clothes gleamed and became whiter than any washing could make them. They saw two other men, Elijah and Moses, speaking with Jesus. Peter's reaction was to say, "Rabbi, how fortunate we are to be here. We can make three shrines – one for you, one for Moses and one for Elijah." Really, he didn't know what to say, for they were terrified. A cloud covered them, and a voice from the cloud said, "This is my Son, and I love him. Listen to him."

They looked round and suddenly they were alone on the mountain with Jesus. As they came down, Jesus commanded them to tell nobody what they had seen, until he had risen from the dead.

from Mark, chapter 8, verse 27 to chapter 9, verse 9

Left
Jesus took Peter, James and John up a high mountain.

The Suffering Messiah
This story records a turning-point in Jesus' ministry. The disciples at last realized that Jesus was the Messiah. Many people hoped that the Messiah would lead a rebellion to drive out the Romans. As soon as the chosen disciples saw that he was the Messiah, Jesus started to teach them that he was not a leader to triumph, but was the Servant Messiah. The prophet Isaiah had foretold of a Servant of God who would bring back God's people by his own suffering and death. The voice at Jesus' baptism had hinted that Jesus was this Servant. He now began to teach his disciples about suffering and service.

The Transfiguration
In their vision the disciples saw Jesus as a heavenly being; this is what the extraordinarily white clothes mean. Jesus was supported by the two great figures of the Old Testament. Moses led the Israelites out of captivity in Egypt; he foretold of a great prophet like himself. The Jews thought that the prophet Elijah would reappear just before the Messiah came. The cloud was the sign of the presence of God. Finally, the voice confirmed that Jesus is God's Son. The disciples who passed down this tradition described in biblical terms their experience of Jesus as the Son of God.

Peter, James and John were suddenly alone with Jesus on the mountain.

Jesus teaching

Like many good teachers, Jesus liked to teach by means of images. His image of God was that of a Jewish daddy (*abba* in Aramaic). His image of hell was *Gehenna*, the huge, foul-smelling rubbish-tip outside Jerusalem, where fires were constantly smouldering. He called himself "the Good Shepherd" and "the Bread of Life". He told his followers that they were "the salt of the earth", and "the light of the world".

This was a traditional way of teaching, much used in the Old Testament, where there are whole books of proverbs such as:

> He takes a stray dog by the ears
> who meddles in someone else's quarrel.

Another favorite way of teaching was by telling stories. When David, the King of Israel, lured away another man's wife and then had the husband killed, his court-prophet Nathan came to him and told him the story of a rich man who took a poor man's only pet lamb to eat. David was furious and threatened judgment on the rich man, so Nathan merely said, "You are the man."

The gospel parables

Jesus set out to make the Kingdom of God a reality on earth. He used images and stories to describe what this Kingdom was like. We do not know in what circumstances Jesus originally told these stories. No doubt he often told them in reply to people who found it hard to accept his message. Or they might ask why Jesus was having so little success; he answered with a story about a king: he invited all his friends to his son's wedding-feast, but when it actually happened they refused to come. Many of Jesus' stories were aimed to convince his hearers that they must make up their minds about him and his message now. The time for decision had come. John the Baptist had used the image of an axe cutting into the roots of a tree. Jesus spoke of a rent-collector arriving to collect his master's rent from the tenants of a vineyard. The tenants beat up the messengers, one after another; so the master would now take the vineyard away.

The Parable of the Sower

One of the stories he taught them was this: "Listen! A farmer went out to sow seed in his field. As he threw the seed from side to side, some fell on the path, where birds came and ate it up. Some fell on rocky ground, where there was not much soil; it sprouted quickly because the soil was shallow, but when the sun came out it withered and died, as it had no roots. Other seed fell among brambles, which grew up and strangled it, so that it produced no grain. Some seed, however, fell on rich soil, and it sprouted and grew, and produced thirty, sixty – even a hundred – times the initial seed sown.

"The farmer sows knowledge about God. The seeds which fell on the path are those people who hear about God, but the Tempter immediately comes and takes away the idea that has been planted in their hearts. Similarly, the seeds which fell on rocky ground are those people who hear the good news and accept it happily. But as soon as they begin to suffer the heat of persecution they lose interest just as quickly, because they have no depth of

Right
A sower scattering grain seed.

faith. Other people are like the seed sown among brambles: they hear about God, but worries, ambition and greed crowd in and strangle their faith, so that it does not achieve anything. Finally, there are those who are sown on rich soil, who hear the gospel and let it change them and then convert others – some thirty, some sixty and some a hundred other people."

from Mark, chapter 4, verses 2–8, 14–20

The sower

Jesus probably told this story when he was reflecting about his mission. In ancient farming plowing was very shallow, done by a donkey pulling one iron point through the rocky ground. Much of the rough ground of Palestine would be impossible to plow up properly. The farmer threw the seed in handfuls from a pouch, with a broad sweep of his hand, and could not control too carefully where the seed fell. Jesus saw that much of his preaching was wasted like seed. The crowds followed him for a short time, but then turned their back on him, and only his small group of disciples stayed loyal. Most of the seed he had sown failed to bear fruit. Only a small part of it produced any grain, but that in enormous quantity.

The parables in the first Christian communities

The detailed explanation which follows the story had special significance for of the first Christian communities. They had the same experiences as Jesus: very few people responded to their message; some gave up very soon, under pressure of persecution or ambition. These were not temptations likely to affect Jesus' first listeners in Galilee; they were much more likely in the cities where Christianity developed, and in the persecutions which Christians suffered later on.

The Parables of the Salt and of the Lamp

Jesus said, "You are the salt of the earth.

Remember that once salt has lost its salty taste, it can never get it back. It's worthless, fit for nothing but to be thrown out where people will walk all over it.

"You are the light of the world. It is impossible to hide a city on a hill. Nobody buys a lamp and then hides it under a measuring basket. They put it on a lamp-stand for all to see! In the same way you too must let your light shine in such a way that people will see the good things you do, and give glory to God."

from Matthew, chapter 5, verses 13–16

Salt and lamps

Most of the salt in Palestine came from the Dead Sea. The River Jordan flows into this sea; in the immense heat it evaporates and forms salt-pans. Only a small quantity of salt is needed to give a new vigor and taste to food. Jesus meant that his disciples, though few in number, were to give a quite new taste to the world.

A normal lamp was a little pottery bowl containing olive-oil, with a lighted wick floating in it. To give good light it had to be put in a prominent position. It would be quite easy to hide the flame under an upturned bowl and prevent any light escaping. Jesus meant that his followers must not be afraid or hide away.

Left
A lamp on a stand.

THE GOOD SAMARITAN

A lawyer stood up and asked Jesus, "Teacher, what must I do to inherit eternal life?" Jesus said to him, "What do the Scriptures say? What do you think?" The man quoted, " 'You shall love the Lord your God with all your heart, soul, strength and mind, and love your neighbour as yourself.' " Jesus said, "That's right! Do that and you will live." The man, to show he knew what he was talking about, said, "Who is my neighbor?"

Jesus replied, "A man was travelling from Jerusalem to Jericho when robbers attacked him, stripped him, beat him and left him half-dead. By chance, a priest was going down the road; he saw the man, but he just passed by. In the same way a temple assistant came along; he saw, but just passed by. But when a certain Samaritan travelling that way saw the man, he felt sorry for him. He bandaged his wounds, pouring oil and wine on them; then he sat him on his own donkey, took him to an inn, and nursed him. Next day he gave two of his own day's wages to the innkeeper, saying, 'Look after him; if it costs more than this, I'll repay you when I return.' "

Jesus asked the lawyer, "Which of the three men was the neighbor of the man attacked by robbers?" The man replied, "The one who cared for him."

"Go and do likewise," said Jesus.
from Luke, chapter 10, verses 25–37

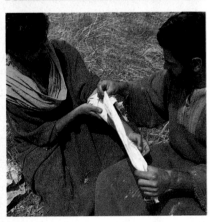

Above
The Samaritan bandaged his wounds having first poured oil and wine on them.

The two commandments

Jewish teachers were often asked to condense the Law in one sentence. One answer given was "Do to others what you would have done to you". The lawyer answered with the great commandment which is the foundation of Judaism, prayed by every faithful Jew three times a day, and called the *Shema* (*Shema* means "Listen!" and it is normally introduced by "Listen, Israel! The Lord your God . . ."). Written very small, it is put as a reminder over every Jewish front-door, and worn in a little box on hands and forehead at the daily prayer.

Jesus liked the lawyer's answer because it put God in the first place. But the reason why the lawyer won special praise is that he saw that the second commandment is linked to the first. Jesus himself taught that genuine love of God must include love of neighbor.

A good neighbor

Jesus did not give answers. He told parables or stories and left the listeners to draw their own conclusions. Only Luke adds the story of the Good Samaritan as an example of the lesson. He wrote his gospel for the Greeks, and often stresses that Jesus came to save all peoples, not only the Jews. As the Jews despised the Samaritans, Jews would be shocked at the story of the two Jews neglecting a fellow-Jew and a despised Samaritan helping him. It also teaches the lesson that to the Christian the well-being of all human beings is important, not only the people from the same background.

The Jewish officials did not know what to do! A dead body was considered unclean from the religious point of view. If the traveller turned out to be dead, they would be made unclean by contact with the corpse. They would miss their turn (which came round quite seldom) to take part in the sacrifices. And, of course, they would not get the pay earned by these duties!

The Samaritan helped the man from the side of the road, put him on his own animal and took him to an inn.

Jesus and sinners

The Jewish teachers of the Law, like many religious people, thought they knew exactly how to win God's favor, whom God liked and whom he disliked. They thought that God had dictated the Jewish Law to Moses, the great leader at the beginning of their people's history. So the Law was God's gift to the Israelites, showing them how to please him and keep close to him. Obedience to the Law should therefore be a joy and a delight for any Jew who loved God.

Right

A woman searching between the rolled bed mats for her lost silver coin.

They found it hard to accept that Jesus was at home with crooks and rogues who did not bother about the Law. They accused him of adopting such standards himself, of being greedy and a drunkard. They knew, of course, what it was to be sorry for not obeying the Law. They expected Jesus to demand that all people should be sorry before he joined up with them. Jesus replied, "It is not the healthy who need the doctor, but the sick." Jesus thought of himself as a doctor to heal sinners; people who thought they weren't sinners thought they didn't need him.

So the gospels recount three stories, one after another, about joy at the return of one who was lost: the lost sheep, the lost coin and the prodigal son.

The Parable of the Lost Sheep

Jesus was surrounded by tax-collectors and all kinds of sinners. Both the Pharisees and the scribes grumbled, saying, "This man welcomes sinners; he even eats with them."

So Jesus told them a parable: "Let's suppose you own a hundred sheep and one of them wanders off. Is there a man among you who doesn't leave the ninety-nine sheep in the pasture and go off looking for the one that got lost, until he finds it?

"Indeed, when he has finally found it, he carries it joyfully home on his shoulders, and calls his friends and neighbors. 'Rejoice with me, for I have found my sheep that I lost,' he says.

"I tell you: in the same way there will be more joy in heaven for one sinner who reforms his ways than for ninety-nine good people who do not need to change."
from Luke, chapter 15, verses 1–7

The Parable of the Lost Coin

Is there a woman who, if she has ten small silver coins but loses one, does not light a lamp, sweep the house and search carefully until she finds it?

"Indeed, when she has found it, she calls together all her friends and neighbors. 'Rejoice with me, for I have found the silver coin I lost,' she tells them.

"I tell you, there is as much joy in heaven when one sinner changes his ways."
from Luke, chapter 15, verses 8–10

The joy of finding

In Jesus' time, most people in the Galilean villages lived permanently in poverty. The single-roomed houses mostly had no windows, and so were dark even in daytime. To find a small coin on the dirt floor, covered in straw and animal dung, would be extremely difficult. So the listeners would understand the care with which the woman searched.

The Lord's Prayer

Once, after Jesus had been praying, one of the disciples said to him, "Lord, teach us how to pray."

Jesus said to them, "When you pray say:

Father, hallowed be your name.

Your kingdom come.

Give us each day our daily bread.

Forgive us our sins,

As we forgive those who sin against us.

And lead us not into temptation."

The Parable of the Visitor at Midnight

Jesus continued and said: "Suppose you have a friend and you go to him at midnight and say to him, 'Lend me three loaves of bread, because another friend has come to stay and I don't have any food for him.' Suppose he answers you from inside his house, 'Leave me alone. I've shut the door and the whole family is in bed. I cannot get up to give you anything.' Even though he won't give you anything for friendship's sake, because you won't stop knocking he will get up and give you whatever you ask.

"So I tell you: ask and it will be given to you. Seek and you will find. Knock, and the door will be opened for you."

from Luke, chapter 11, verses 1–9

The importance of hospitality

Most Jews in the time of Jesus went to bed when it grew dark. They gathered their animals into the house, then barred and bolted the door. Most houses consisted of one room only. If it was too cold to sleep on the roof, the family would sleep on a raised platform at the back of the room. They slept together on a large mat, with the children nearest to the edge of the platform (and to the animals). The head of the family slept against the far wall. To go and open the door would involve climbing over the entire family and pushing through all the animals – and in the pitch dark.

As often with Luke's parables, there is a witty side to this: the householder does the right thing for the wrong reason. To the Jews it is always a disgrace to refuse hospitality. If the householder carried on refusing, the noise would wake the whole village, and they would know he had refused to help.

It is a mistake to think that every point in Jesus' stories has a lesson. God is not a lazy friend who is spurred into action only by fear of being shamed. Each of these stories had just one point: carry on praying, even if the prayer is not granted at first!

The person who prays persistently in the parable reflects Jesus' own way of prayer. In Luke's gospel especially, Jesus prayed before every important moment: at the baptism, after his first healing miracle, before choosing his special Twelve, before the transfiguration, and so on. Especially, as in the garden before his passion, he taught his disciples to pray when they were in difficulties.

Right
The family asleep at night on their mats cover the floor of their house.

THE PRODIGAL SON

Jesus told his disciples this story: "A man had two sons. The younger son said to his father, 'Father, give me my share of the estate now.' So the man divided his property between his two sons. Not long afterwards the younger son collected all his belongings and went to a far-off country, where he wasted his wealth in wild living. When he had spent everything, however, the country suffered a severe famine and he became destitute. He got work with one of the local people, who gave him a job feeding the pigs. No one gave him anything; he would have been glad to eat even the bean pods in the pig-swill.

"He thought to himself: my father's farm-hands have as much food as they can eat, and here I am starving to death with hunger! I will go home to my father, and I will say to him, 'Father, I have sinned against God and against you. I am no longer fit to be called your son; employ me as a farm-hand.' He got up and went home. His father saw him in the distance and felt sorry for him; he ran to his son, hugged him and kissed him over and over again. The son started to say the speech he had rehearsed, but the father called the servants. 'Hurry! Give him my best robe. Put a ring on his finger and sandals on his feet. Bring the calf and prepare it. We'll have a feast, for here is my son – alive and well.' They all began to celebrate.

"The elder son, however, had been working in the fields. When he came near the house, he heard the sound of music and dancing, and asked a servant what was happening. When he was told that his father had killed the prize calf because his brother was back, he was furious and refused to go in, even when his father kept begging him. 'Look here! I've been your slave all these years. I did all you ever asked. You never even killed a goat so I could feast with my friends. But this son of yours turns up, having wasted all your wealth on prostitutes, and you kill the fatted calf for him,' he said.

"The father answered, 'My son, you are always here with me, and everything I own is yours. It is right to be happy, for it is as though your brother was dead, but now he is alive; he was lost, but we have found him.' "

from Luke, chapter 15, verses 11–32

The father recognizes his younger son, whom he had thought lost, in the distance and runs to welcome him home.

The wastrel
The younger son has no right to any property till his father is dead, and by law is obliged to support his father in his old age. Yet he wastes his father's money. He looks after pigs, to Jews unclean animals, and so is contaminated by them.

The worker
He is no better! In a fury, he insults his father, refuses to come to the feast. He shouts "Look here!" without calling him "Father". He refuses to acknowledge his brother. He assumes that his brother has spent the money on prostitutes, a disgrace in Jewish society in which respect for family loyalty is all-important.

The father
He is so keen to have the younger son back that he throws all dignity away by running to greet him. He brushes aside the pretty prepared speech, shows his acceptance and trust by clothing him in his own robe, and lays on a feast for him. But he also offers forgiveness to the elder son, turning a deaf ear to the insults, and only gently reminding him that the returning son is also "your brother".

Overleaf
Jesus had compassion on the ten lepers and told them to go and show themselves to the priest.

JESUS HEALS THE LEPERS

Jesus set out for Jerusalem. Ten lepers met him as he was about to enter a village on the border between Galilee and Samaria. They kept their distance and shouted, "Jesus, Master, take pity on us!" Seeing them, Jesus told them, "Go to the priests to be examined." As they went, they were cleansed of their leprosy.

One of them, when he saw that he was cured, returned, praising God with a loud voice. He threw himself down at Jesus' feet and thanked him.

Now this man was a Samaritan. Jesus said to him, "Were there not ten men who were cleansed of leprosy? Where are the other nine? Did nobody come back to praise God except this foreigner? Get up and go away. Your trust has made you well."

from Luke, chapter 17, verses 11–19

Above

A lepers' cave where they lived separated from the community.

Laws about leprosy

Many of the Old Testament Laws of purity have both a symbolic and practical significance. Some are based on basic principles of medicine and hygiene that still make sense today.

The Laws covering leprosy were designed to prevent diseases from spreading – but at a heavy price. "Leprosy" covered many diseases, including skin-diseases, ringworm, dry-rot and mildew. "Leprosy" could happen in clothes and buildings, too. Priests had to issue certificates that someone who had once been contaminated was now clear of the disease. Lepers were kept in isolation from the community and had to warn anyone who strayed near them. Any person who touched them was contaminated. So they lived a pitiful, uncared-for and lonely existence, beyond the boundary of any towns or villages without hope of cure or recovery.

Jesus obviously pitied these unfortunate people, showing his care and affection by actually touching them, in defiance of Law and danger. The number of times Jesus healed lepers shows there were many of them in Palestine. Healing of lepers was also one of the signs of the coming of God's Kingdom prophesied by Isaiah.

Luke's account of the healing of the lepers contains one of his favorite themes: that Jesus came to save those rejected by others.

Luke especially emphasizes Jesus' welcome to outcasts of all kinds. Jesus welcomes sinners, even prostitutes, the poor, the crippled, women. In those days women had an inferior position, even among educated people. Luke carefully shows Jesus' special consideration towards them.

Thanks

The Samaritan's joy as he strides along, calling out in his delight, is typical of Luke. He always emphasizes joy and cheerfulness in the way in which people thank God, praise him, glorify him when they have seen and felt his power at work. The shepherds at Jesus' birth go home glorifying and praising God, too.

Below

A crutch for the crippled among the lepers.

JESUS WELCOMES CHILDREN

Some people brought their children to Jesus, so he might give them a blessing. The disciples turned them away.

When Jesus saw this, however, he was angry and said to them, "Let the children come to me. Don't stop them. God's kingdom consists of people like them.

Amen I say to you, if you do not receive God's kingdom like a child you will not enter it under any circumstances."

Then he hugged the children, put his hands upon their heads, and gave them a blessing.

from Mark, chapter 10, verses 13–16

The children of Palestine

To Jews the family is very important, and children are regarded as a blessing. But children are strictly brought up, with special attention to the commandment, "Honor your father and your mother." In the Scriptures the Book of Proverbs advises, "Correct your child and your child will give you peace of mind, will delight your soul." Children remained strictly separate from adults, so presumably the disciples thought Jesus did not want to be bothered with them.

But Jesus here put children forward as models. Why? Perhaps he meant to praise the openness and enthusiasm of children. Perhaps he meant that his followers needed to rely on their Father in heaven as young children rely on their parents.

The anger of Jesus

Jesus was not always "gentle Jesus, meek and mild". It is striking that he did not lose his temper at insults to himself. He did not react at all to the sarcasm and sharpness of the disciples towards him. But there was surely some exasperation in his repeated questions to the disciples, "Do you still not understand, still not realize?" So when the disciples pushed the children away he showed his annoyance, not a loss of temper, but certainly a stirring of emotion. On another occasion he was criticized for healing on the sabbath and "he looked angrily round at them, grieved to find them so obstinate".

The sabbath

The sabbath was the day on which no work was allowed. Even lifting or carrying or cutting food was counted as work. If death threatened exceptions were made. The sabbath began at sunset on Friday and all food for Saturday had to be ready by then.

Amen, amen

Like *abba*, *amen* is an Aramaic word characteristic of Jesus' own speech, recorded here in Aramaic although the gospel is written in Greek. It must have had the familiar ring of the Master's own words. The basic meaning of the word is *truth, firmness, solidity*. "Amen, amen," said Jesus, before a saying he wished especially to emphasize as true. God is reliable and faithful above all things: "Christ, the *Amen* of God, is this reliability and faithfulness," says Paul. In the Old Testament, when a blessing or a curse was read out, the people cried, "*Amen*," as though to say "So be it or it is the truth."

So to the Christian **Amen** is an affirmation of the prayer's truthfulness and a commitment of the prayer to God.

ZACCHAEUS THE TAX-COLLECTOR

On his way to Jerusalem, Jesus passed through Jericho. A man called Zacchaeus (who was the chief tax-collector and a very rich man) tried to get a look at Jesus. Zacchaeus was a little man, and he couldn't see Jesus over the heads of the crowd. So he ran ahead and climbed a sycamore tree to get a better look as Jesus passed by. When he reached him, Jesus looked up and said, "Zacchaeus, come down quickly. I have to visit your house today." Delighted, Zacchaeus scrambled down, and took Jesus into his home.

When they saw what had happened, everybody grumbled, saying, "He's gone to visit a sinner!" Zacchaeus, however, stood up and said to the Lord, "Look, Lord, I will give half my possessions to the poor, and if I have taken too much tax from anyone, I will pay him back four times as much as I took." Jesus told him, "Today you and your family have been saved because you are a son of Abraham too! For the Son of Man came to seek and save people who are lost."

from Luke, chapter 19, verses 1–10

Jesus looked up to where Zacchaeus, the tax-collector was in the tree.

Jericho

Jericho, "the city of ten thousand palm trees", is one of the oldest cities in the world; it has a stone-tower built in 6000 BC. Its great warmth (in the Jordan Valley at 300 metres below sea-level) and plentiful springs make it ideal for agriculture. Oranges, melons, dates, bananas grow there in abundance. On Jesus' journey it would have been the last city of the Jordan Valley. After that he turned into the hills, past King Herod's winter palace, heading up to Jerusalem, four hours' walk away. This was the last stop on his great journey to Jerusalem and his crucifixion.

Tax-collectors

Like any government with many officials and a large army, Rome imposed heavy taxes. The rich and the merchants could afford to pay these taxes, passing the expense on to others. But the poor had no tax-relief and must have found it hard. Tax-collecting was a business matter: the right to collect taxes was auctioned to the highest bidder, and a successful bidder kept any profits. Zacchaeus may well have bought the right to collect the taxes of Jericho, and made sure he did not lose by it! In addition tax-collectors were unpopular because they worked for the detested Roman occupiers; tax-collectors were outcasts from any decent Jewish society. They lost their Jewish identity and sided with the occupying power.

So Zacchaeus was an outcast. Jesus himself took the initiative and invited himself to the sinner's house. He did not wait till the sinner had first expressed repentance or willingness to receive him. Jesus made the first move, and left Zacchaeus no choice: "I have to visit your house," he said.

But the whole-heartedness of Zacchaeus' repentence was shown by his generosity. The Jewish Law imposed fourfold restitution only for the theft and slaughter (or sale) of cattle. The normal penalty was one-fifth above the offence.

178

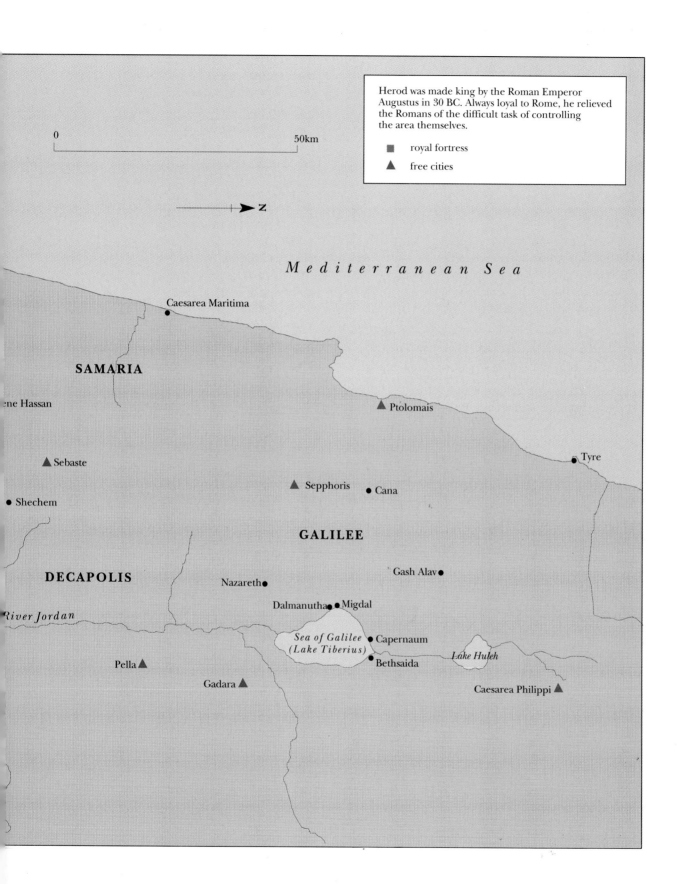

Herod was made king by the Roman Emperor Augustus in 30 BC. Always loyal to Rome, he relieved the Romans of the difficult task of controlling the area themselves.

■ royal fortress

▲ free cities

0   50km

Z

Mediterranean Sea

Caesarea Maritima

SAMARIA

ene Hassan

▲ Ptolomais

● Tyre

▲ Sebaste

▲ Sepphoris   ● Cana

● Shechem

GALILEE

DECAPOLIS

Gash Alav ●

Nazareth ●

River Jordan

Dalmanutha ● ● Migdal

*Sea of Galilee
(Lake Tiberius)*   ● Capernaum

Lake Huleh

Pella ▲

● Bethsaida

Gadara ▲

Caesarea Philippi ▲

183

Jesus approached Jerusalem. When he saw the city, he wept over it.

He said, "If only you had known the way to peace! But at the moment you cannot see what you have to do. For the days are coming when your enemies will build ramps up against your walls. They will besiege you and attack you from every side, and raze you to the ground. Your children will be cut down. Not one stone will be left standing on another – because you did not realize that God had come to you."

from Luke, chapter 19, verses 41–44

Passion week

Jesus spent most of his life in Galilee. The Gospel of John mentions occasional visits to Jerusalem throughout Jesus' ministry but the other gospels only report on his activities in Jerusalem in the final week.

In Jerusalem Jesus' activity entered into a new phase. In Galilee he had concentrated on proclaiming the Kingship of God. He had had several clashes with the Pharisees, the strict interpreters of the Law. They considered that a loyal response to God's Law involved keeping every little detail, including the complicated interpretations handed down by former teachers. They disapproved of many of Jesus' attitudes to the Law. He often cut through a tangle of meanings drawn out of the Law, to return to its original purpose. This was his way of renewing the Jewish religion, bringing the Kingship of God to its fulfilment. His behavior upset and annoyed the Pharisees, but it would not have led to

Left
A hillside of model houses in Jerusalem.

any fatal clash. Such interpretations of the Law were not considered sacrilegious.

But when Jesus came to Jerusalem, his renewal of Judaism took on a different form. Jesus first made a demonstration against the worship in the Temple. He needed to show that this worship, with its quantities of animal sacrifice, must be swept aside and a new kind of worship take its place. This brought him into immediate conflict with the Sadducees, the guardians of the Temple.

The Sadducees
The Sadducees were the families of the chief priests. From their number the high priest himself was chosen. The high priest was the chief local ruler, though still subject to the Roman governor. The Sadducees were interested above all in keeping their own political and religious position secure.

The Pharisees
The Pharisees seem to have been rather timid, not men of action, and always wanting some previous authority to justify their actions; they lacked initiative and decisiveness. But the aristocratic and politically minded Sadducees were of a different stamp. They were not afraid of acting decisively to defend their position. They demanded to know Jesus' authority for his actions in the Temple. This led on to several controversies between them and Jesus.

A dangerous time
As the great festival of the Passover approached, when there were large crowds in Jerusalem, the Sadducees were determined to get rid of Jesus. They had to be careful to avoid any demonstration which might spread to a mass movement, and so upset their position with the Roman governors. If Jesus decided to make another demonstration in front of the great crowds, the crowds might respond enthusiastically, and a revolt occur. They could not risk that, and so must get rid of Jesus before the feast began.

The Messiah's rejection
For Jesus the failure of Jerusalem to accept his message was the final tragedy. The Gospel of Luke especially shows the importance of this final journey to Jerusalem: Jesus came from Galilee, teaching on the way, and all the time aware of his goal, the Holy City. Then, as he came near, he was hailed by the crowds: "Blessed is he who comes in the name of the Lord. Peace on earth and glory in the highest." They echoed the words of the angels to the shepherds. But Jerusalem did not accept the message, and Jesus wept over the city as he looked down on it from the Mount of Olives.

Jerusalem
From the mount of the olive-trees Jerusalem is still an unforgettable sight, white roofs shimmering in the heat across the narrow valley, the magnificent esplanade of the Temple dominating the landscape. In Jesus' day there were also the ten great bronze doors and the gilded roof of the Temple itself, a breath-taking view – all to be destroyed.

THE ENTRY TO JERUSALEM

They drew near to Jerusalem. When they had reached Bethphage near to the mountain of the olive-trees, Jesus sent two of the disciples on ahead. He told them, "Go to the next village. You will immediately find a donkey tied up there, and her foal with her. Untie them and bring them to me. If anyone asks you what you are doing, tell him, 'The Lord needs them.' He will let you have them."

All this happened so that the prophecy might come true: "Tell the daughter of Zion, 'Behold! Your king comes to you, humbly riding on a donkey, on the foal of an animal used for carrying.' "

The disciples did as Jesus told them and brought the donkey and the foal. They draped their outer clothes over them and Jesus got on. Most of the crowd spread their outer clothes on the road; others cut branches from the trees and scattered them in his path. The crowd in front of Jesus and behind him shouted, "Hosanna to the son of David! Blessed be he who comes in the name of the Lord God! Hosanna in the highest places!"

The whole city was in an uproar when he entered Jerusalem. "Who is he?" everybody was asking. "He is Jesus, the prophet from Nazareth in Galilee," answered the crowds.
from Matthew, chapter 21, verses 1–11

The claim to be the Messiah

Jesus came into Jerusalem as just one among a crowd of pilgrims. They were all coming up for the feast, waving palm-branches and singing a royal psalm, as was normal at some feasts. After the resurrection the disciples looked back on the scene and realised that this event was Jesus' entry into Jerusalem as king. They remembered afterwards that the Jewish prophets had foretold that the Messiah would enter Jerusalem as a humble king, riding on a donkey, and saw it as a significant event in Jesus' life. A donkey is a very delicate and graceful animal, and in ancient times kings often rode on donkeys. They saw the palms and hymns for the feast as special homage to Jesus, and the crowds as his own retinue.

Hosanna

Hosanna is a Hebrew word that has passed into English through Greek and Latin. Many Hebrew words have passed into English. For instance, "Jeremy" is an English form of what began as *Yir-me-yahu*. Many other names also end in *Yahu*, the short form of the Hebrew name of God, *Yahweh*. Hebrew names normally have a meaning. So "Jesus" is an English form of *Yehoshua* ("Yahweh saves"); it is the same word as "Joshua". In the same way *Hosanna* is simplified from the Hebrew *hosiyah-na*, and originally was a cry for help, meaning "Save, please!" In fact it became a joyful shout, like "Hurrah!"

The Liberator

The crowds in Jerusalem were wondering whether Jesus was going to lead a revolution against the Romans. The Jews hated foreign domination so much that there were several attempts at rebellion. In AD 66 a full-scale rebellion broke out, and the Romans besieged Jerusalem for four years. They eventually sacked it and devastated the Temple.

Jesus riding on a donkey entered Jerusalem.

186

CLEANSING THE TEMPLE

Jesus went into the Temple and began to throw out all those who were buying and selling. He overturned the tables of the money-changers and the chairs of those who were selling doves, and would not let anyone carry anything through the Temple courtyards. He taught them, "Doesn't it say in the Scriptures: 'My house shall be called a House of Prayer for people of all races'? You people have turned it into a robbers' cave."

When the high priests and the scribes heard about this, they began looking for a way to destroy Jesus. They were afraid of him, because the crowds were amazed at his teaching.

from Mark, chapter 11, verses 15–18

Above

The money-changers in the Temple used scales to check the weight of the coins.

The Temple in Jerusalem

The Temple built by Herod was a magnificent building, the splendor of the eastern Mediterranean, and possibly the grandest construction anywhere in the world at this time. In the centre of the huge paved courtyard was the Holy of Holies, closed by a magnificent tapestry curtain. Here only the high priest entered once a year, to ask God's pardon for all the offences of the people. Around this building was a series of courtyards: first, the Court of the Priests, then the Court of Israel (for male Jews only), the Court of the Women (for any Jew) and finally the Court of the Gentiles. For a Gentile to pass beyond the Court of the Gentiles was an offence punishable by death. A Roman soldier was once executed for relieving himself against the wall of the Court when he was stationed outside it on guard-duty.

Money-changers

Every city-state round the Mediterranean had its own coinage, stamped as a guarantee that it contained so much silver. Some cities cheated and saved silver by mixing in cheaper metals. One of the most reliable coinages was that of Tyre. Only Tyrian coinage was accepted in the Temple, so that pilgrims with other coinages had to change their money.

Animal sacrifice

Animal sacrifices were among the most common in the Temple, though there were also sacrifices of wheat and fruit. It was awkward to bring your own animals, which might not survive the journey intact, and anyway, pilgrims were expected to spend a certain amount of money in Jerusalem – a sort of holy holiday fund. It was too messy to keep the larger animals in the Temple precincts, but bird-droppings could be confined to their cages or baskets and not render the building "unclean".

Jesus in the Temple

Jesus' action in the Temple was not a cleansing of minor abuses. It was a sign of the renewal of Judaism, a sign that a whole new way of worshipping God was needed. He had come to get rid of the old ways and to make a new People of Israel. God's Temple was to be a house of prayer for all nations, not just the Jews.

Artists sometimes represent Jesus' action as wholesale and angry devastation. There is no reason to suppose that he lost his temper, and if the action had been on a large scale he would surely have been arrested by the Temple police on the spot. It was a symbolic action, like those of the Old Testament prophets.

Jesus overturned the tables of the money-changers and the chairs of those selling doves.

JESUS WASHES HIS DISCIPLES' FEET

Jesus realized that his hour had come when he would leave this world and return to the Father. Having always loved his chosen followers, he loved them to the end. The Tempter had already put the idea of betraying Jesus into the heart of Judas Iscariot, one of the twelve disciples.

Jesus knew that God had given him power over all things. He knew that he came from God, and was going to God. He got up from the table, took off his outer clothes and tied a towel round himself. Then he poured water into a basin and began to wash the disciples' feet, drying them with the towel. When he came to Simon Peter, Peter said to him, "Lord, are you going to wash my feet? I'll never ever let you wash my feet."

Jesus answered, "Unless I wash you, you will not share in my inheritance."

When he had finished washing their feet he put his outer clothes back on. Returning to the table he asked them, "Do you know what I have done to you? You call me 'Lord' and 'Teacher' – quite rightly, for that is what I am. So if I, your 'Lord' and 'Teacher', have washed your feet, you also have a duty to wash each other's feet. I have set you an example; as I have done to you, so you must do to others."

from John, chapter 13, verses 1–8, 12–15

Overleaf

When the hour came Jesus took his place at the table.

Judas Iscariot

The gospels do not fully explain why Judas betrayed Jesus. Mark simply describes how he sold Jesus for money. Luke says that Satan entered into him. John adds that he was also a thief, who was stealing from the disciples' petty cash. His name may be a clue, for "Judas" was a name popular with the nationalist party who fought for the liberation of the Jews from Rome. Perhaps Judas thought Jesus would be a freedom-fighter, and was disillusioned when he saw that Jesus was not a political liberator. "Iscariot" may mean simply "man from Kariot" (the village of Kariot) or could mean "man of the purse", which would fit John's statement. The gospels stress the horror of his treachery: he had not only shared a meal with Jesus just beforehand, but had actually demonstrated the closest friendship by sharing the same plate of food.

The Servant of Others

The washing of the disciples' feet was an acted parable: Jesus showed once again that he was the suffering Servant prophesied by Isaiah, who would lay down his life in the service of others.

All Jewish people wore open-toed sandals. Roads were dry, dusty and stony. In a town like Jerusalem the roads would be especially foul, for the narrow streets were also the drains. Travellers' feet would become sore and dirty after even a short journey. It was an act of hospitality to have your visitor's feet washed. But it was considered so humiliating to wash someone's dirty feet that a Jewish slave could not be asked to do it; only a Gentile slave, called a "dog" by the Jews, would be ordered to do it.

He loved them to the end

Several Greek words are translated by the English word "love": *eros* is sexual love between man and woman; *philia* is the love of one friend for another; *agape* was used for this new Christian love which serves others, no matter what the cost. It is a thoughtful and generous love, such as members of the same family have for each other, when they are prepared to come to the rescue in real need and at real cost.

Jesus got up from the table and washed the disciples' feet.

THE LAST SUPPER

The Day of Unleavened Bread came, when the Passover lamb had to be sacrificed. Jesus sent out Peter and John with these orders: "Listen! As you go into Jerusalem, you will see a man carrying a jar of water. Follow him. When he goes into the house, say to the householder, 'The Teacher asks, "Where is the guest-room where the disciples and I can eat the Passover meal?"'' He will show you a large furnished upper-room; prepare the meal there." They went, and everything happened as Jesus had said, and they prepared all they needed.

When the hour came, Jesus and the twelve apostles lay round the table. He said, "I really wanted to eat a Passover meal with you before I have to suffer, for I tell you, I will never eat it again until God's kingdom has come." He took a cup and gave thanks to God, saying, "Take this and share it out between you. I tell you, I will never drink wine again until God's kingdom has come."

Then he took a loaf of bread, gave thanks to God, broke it, and gave it to them, saying, "This is my body which is given for you. Do this in remembrance of me." After the meal, he took the cup saying, "This cup is my blood which is poured out for you. It marks a new contract between God and man.

"But listen! A traitor is at this table with me. The Son of Man goes to his destiny, but it will be terrible for the man who has betrayed him."

from Luke, chapter 22, verses 7–22

Above
*The Passover food:
wine, bitter herbs,
roast lamb and
unleavened bread.*

The Jewish Passover

The Passover was the great feast of the Jews, celebrating the escape of the Jews from Egypt under Moses, and the forty years in the desert, when God formed the people of Israel as his own.

The disciples' preparations were special. In this case, Jesus told them to follow a man carrying a water-jar. This would be as conspicuous as a man carrying a lady's umbrella – for only women carried water-jars. The story has an air of mystery and destiny: they don't quite know what it all means. They "lay" around the low table, all facing inwards, sitting on rugs and propped on an elbow.

At the feast itself, there was a fixed routine, with wine, salty herbs (the bitter salt reminded the eaters how bitter the captivity in Egypt had been), roast lamb and unleavened bread. The climax was when a young child asked the father of the family why this night was different and why they had red wine. The answer was, "It is a reminder of the blood of the lamb which Moses told our ancestors to put on the doorposts at the escape from Egypt."

The covenant

Jesus intended this moment to seal a new agreement between God and humanity. The Jews believed that God had made a contract – a sort of marriage contract – with Israel in the desert in the time of Moses, making them his own special people. That first contract had been sealed by the sacrifice of an animal, a lamb; this new contract would be sealed by the sacrifice of Jesus. He knew the Temple authorities would soon act to kill him. He regarded himself as a lamb sacrificed for the good of the people.

Christians celebrate the story of the Last Supper in the act of worship called the Mass, the Communion Service, the Eucharist, or the Lord's Supper.

IN THE GARDEN OF GETHSEMANE

Jesus and his disciples went to a place called Gethsemane, the Garden of Olives. There he said to his disciples, "Stay here while I pray." He took Peter with him, and James and John. He was agitated and distressed, and said to them, "A sadness like death is sweeping over my soul. Stay awake and keep watch." He went a little way on and threw himself on the ground and prayed that, if it was possible, he might avoid the time of suffering. He prayed, "*Abba*, Father, you can do anything. If it is possible, take this cup from me. Nevertheless, not what I want, but what you want." He returned to his disciples, and found them asleep. He said to Peter, "Simon, are you asleep? Couldn't you stay awake one hour? Stay awake and pray that you will not be tested. The spirit is willing, but the flesh is weak."

He went away again, praying in the same words as before. When he returned, however, he found them still sleeping; they could not keep their eyes open. They offered no excuse.

When he came the third time, he said to them, "Are you still asleep and having a rest? It's over! The time is here.

Left
Gethsemane was a garden of olive trees.

Look! The Son of Man is betrayed into the hands of sinners. Get up! Let's go! The traitor is coming."

Immediately, while he was speaking, Judas, one of the twelve disciples, arrived with a great crowd of men, sent by the chief priests, scribes and Jewish elders. They were armed with swords and clubs. The traitor had given them a sign: "The man I kiss is the one. Arrest him and take him away safely." He went straight over to Jesus and said, "Rabbi!" and he gave him a kiss of friendship. Then they took hold of Jesus and arrested him.

A certain bystander drew his sword and cut off the ear of the high priest's slave. Jesus, however, said, "Am I a terrorist, that you need swords and clubs? I've been teaching in the Temple every day, but you didn't arrest me there – the prophecies in the Scriptures have come true." Then the disciples all left him and ran away. A certain young man, wearing nothing but a sheet, followed Jesus. They seized him too, but he left the sheet, and ran off naked.

from Mark, chapter 14, verses 32–52

Jesus faces death
Jesus must have known that he was risking his life. He had challenged the authorities by his action in the Temple, and they would want to remove any chance of him doing it again in front of the Passover crowds.

On Passover night pilgrims were meant to stay in Jerusalem. But the crowds were such

that the hill opposite was counted as part of the city, and many camped there.

No one has identified the man wearing a sheet. Was it the author of the gospel?

The arresting party
The different gospel-writers do not make clear who arrested Jesus, whether it was Jews or the Romans.

Overleaf
Judas brought with him a detachment of soldiers and the Temple police.

PETER DENIES JESUS

Right
A high priest.

On the way to Gethsemane, Jesus had predicted that, before the rooster crowed, Peter would three times deny that he knew him. After Jesus' arrest, Peter followed the crowd to the high priest's house, where Jesus was being questioned.

Peter was sitting out in the courtyard. One of the high priest's housemaids came and said to him, "You were with Jesus of Nazareth!" But he denied it in front of them all, saying, "I do not know what you are saying." He went out into the gateway, where another maid-servant saw him and said to the men there, "He was with Jesus of Nazareth." Peter swore that it wasn't true: "I do not know the man."

After a while, however, the bystanders said to Peter, "Surely you're one of them; your dialect gives you away." Then Peter began to curse and swear, "I do not know the man!" Immediately the rooster crowed. Peter remembered what Jesus had said: "Before the rooster crows, you will three times deny that you know me." And he went out and wept bitterly.

from Matthew, chapter 26, verses 69–75

Peter the Brave!

Peter was always full of bluster and good intentions. He had the courage to go into the courtyard of the high priest's palace. Then he was scared off by this young girl – and the Greek word translated as "housemaid" above really means "little child". His countryman's accent was immediately obvious. Judaeans despised and teased Galileans for their distinctive northern accent. There was an old biblical story about testing people to see what area of the country they came from by pronouncing the Hebrew for "ear of grain": those east of the Jordan said *shibboleth*, and those west of the Jordan said *sibboleth*.

The gospel-writer brings out the tragedy of the contrast between Peter and Jesus: Jesus stands his ground before the high priest, his leading disciple is frightened into disowning him.

The interrogation of Jesus

The high priest was the native ruler of Judaea, a political force as well as a religious one, though the Roman governor had final control of the province. The Roman governor made final decisions about taxes, about war and peace, and about any matter involving a Roman citizen. He could also remove the high priest from office. At this time the high priest was called Caiaphas, but the real power seems to have been held by his father-in-law, Annas. Annas had himself been high priest. The Romans removed him from office, but several of his sons and sons-in-law became high priests, and in fact Annas continued to exercise power through them.

As long as they paid taxes and prevented rebellions, the Romans usually allowed local councils or noblemen to administer the provinces. They would pass regulations about trade and land-rights, and could judge most lawsuits. But no local ruler could pass a death sentence. So the high priest had to prepare a charge against Jesus which would persuade the Roman governor to condemn Jesus as a rebel leader. The governor held his court early in the morning, so they had to prepare the charge that night.

Peter was in the gateway of the high priest's house when a maid-servant saw him and said, "He was with Jesus of Nazareth."

BEFORE PONTIUS PILATE

Pontius Pilate washed his hands of the decision to crucify Jesus.

At dawn, the chief priests and Jewish leaders held a meeting to decide how they could have Jesus put to death. They put him in chains and took him to Pontius Pilate, the Roman governor. "Do you really claim to be the King of the Jews?" asked Pilate. "If you say so," Jesus said.

Jesus made no reply to the accusations of the chief priests and Jewish leaders. "Don't you hear what they are saying about you?" Pilate said to Jesus. Much to his surprise and admiration, Jesus still refused to answer.

Every year, during the festival of the Passover, it was Pilate's custom to release a prisoner; the choice was left to the Jewish people. This year he had in prison a well-known criminal called Barabbas. When a crowd had gathered, Pilate asked them, "Which man should I set free – Barabbas, or Jesus called the Christ?" Pilate realized that the Jewish authorities had arrested Jesus only because they hated him.

Below
Rods were symbols of a Roman consul's authority.

The chief priests and Jewish leaders, however, whipped up the crowd to ask for Barabbas to be released. "What, then, do you want me to do with Jesus, who is called the Christ?" asked Pilate. "Crucify him!" they replied. "Why? What has he done wrong?' asked Pilate. But all they would answer was to shout fiercely, "Crucify him!" When Pilate saw that a riot was about to start, he had a bowl of water brought to him. There, in front of them all, he washed his hands of the whole affair and said, "I am not responsible for this man's death."

from Matthew, chapter 27, verses 1–24

A weak and puzzled governor

Judaea was only a small territory of the Roman Empire, so it was ruled by a prefect. He was responsible for peace in the country and for the protection of Roman citizens and Roman trade there. But the Jews hated Roman rule, and made life as difficult as possible for the Roman governors. They complained to the emperor that they were being harshly treated! Pontius Pilate put up an inscription to the emperor, and they complained that it was sacrilegious in the Holy City of Jerusalem. He built a water supply for Jerusalem and they refused to allow the funds of the Holy City to pay for it. Both these incidents made him look incompetent. Eventually, in AD 36, he was dismissed for cruelty when he killed some rioters in a rebellion.

Pilate saw that the charge against Jesus was unproven. But the emperor was particularly fierce against anyone suspected of rebellion. Pilate did not dare risk the emperor's anger by acquitting a prisoner accused of being a rebel leader.

The amnesty

At the time of the Passover the Jews celebrated the time when Moses set them free from their slavery in Egypt. During the festival the Romans set a Jewish prisoner free. It was merely a gesture, but this time it gave Pilate the opportunity to try to set Jesus free. The Jerusalem crowds were easily persuaded by the Temple authorities to shout for a popular freedom-fighter, Barabbas. In the end, Pilate just abandoned his attempt to have justice done and gave way. He was not prepared to risk his job to save one religious teacher.

Above
All records and books in Roman times were written on scrolls.

201

SCOURGING AND MOCKING

Below
A Roman whip.

Pilate set Barabbas free, then he ordered that Jesus be scourged, and handed him over to be crucified.

The governor's soldiers led Jesus to the *praetorium*. The whole cohort gathered round him. They stripped him and hung a soldier's scarlet *chlamys* on him. They wove an acanthus branch into a crown and placed it on his head, and put a stick in his right hand. Then they knelt before him and mocked him, saying, "Hail, King of the Jews!" They spat on him, and then they took the stick from him and hit him on the head with it.

When they had finished laughing at Jesus, they took off the *chlamys*, put his own clothes back on him and led him out to be crucified.

from Matthew, chapter 27, verses 26–31

Jesus was scourged and mocked by soldiers.

The soldiers

Soldiers were stationed at two places in Jerusalem. There was a permanent garrison at the Fortress Antonia, overlooking the Temple. There they could spot a riot or any trouble developing before it got dangerous. Normally the Roman governor was stationed at Caesarea, the capital of Palestine. This was a port on the coast, built by King Herod and named after his friend and patron, Augustus Caesar. For the great festivals, however, the governor himself came up to make sure there were no disturbances. The extra troops he brought lodged with him in the ancient citadel and royal palace, whose three massive towers still stand today.

Right
Thorns twisted into a crown.

The scourging

There were two distinct forms of beating. Luke says that Pilate suggested during the trial that Jesus should merely be beaten – a slighter punishment to warn a prisoner not to repeat an offence. But the full-scale flogging which Matthew reports was a different matter. It was often part of the torture of crucifixion, but in this case it seems that Pilate gave special orders that it should be done. The victim was stripped and tied to a post so that he was bent double, then he was lashed with a short-handled whip. Sharp pieces of lead or spikes were attached to the leather thongs, and the wounds inflicted were so severe that men often died from the scourging alone.

The mockery

The execution was not to take place immediately. To fill in the time the whole detachment gathered; this would have been several hundred men. As Jesus had been condemned for claiming to be king, they proceeded to make fun of him as king. The *chlamys* was a short military cloak of scarlet wool, fastened at the shoulder with a clasp. Sometimes an expensive version would be presented to foreign kings. The stick put into his right hand was the sign of authority, perhaps the vine-wood rod carried by a centurion (a military officer).

The crown of thorns is usually represented as modelled on the laurel wreath worn by Roman emperors. But eastern kings wore a sort of jewelled turban. This would be easier to make: they needed only to take a pile of thorny brushwood and put it on his head as a crown. The mockery was completed by kneeling before the tortured figure and crying, "Hail, King of the Jews!" just as people knelt before the emperor and cried, "Hail, Caesar."

THE CRUCIFIXION

It was nine o'clock
in the morning when
they crucified
Jesus.

Jesus was taken out to be crucified. On the way the soldiers forced a man called Simon, from Cyrene in North Africa, to carry the cross. A pain-killer of wine drugged with myrrh was offered to Jesus, but he refused to drink it.

At nine o'clock in the morning, Jesus was crucified. The soldiers on duty gambled for his clothes. The notice explaining the charge against him read, "The King of the Jews". Two robbers were crucified with him, one on either side of him.

The passers-by hurled insults, especially the chief priests and the scribes. They jeered, "He saved others, but he cannot save himself! The Christ! The King of Israel! If he came down from the cross right now, we might believe in him."

During the three hours after noon, the sky grew dark. Then at three o'clock Jesus shouted out in the Aramaic language, "*Eloi, Eloi, lama sabachthani?*" (meaning, "My God, my God, why have you forsaken me?"). Some bystanders said, "He is calling the prophet Elijah." One man ran and soaked a sponge in cheap wine. He put it on the end of a stick and held it to Jesus' lips. "Leave him be; perhaps Elijah is coming to take him down from the cross," he said.

With a loud cry Jesus died. The centurion in charge of the crucifixion saw him die. "Truly this man was the son of God," he said. Many women who had followed Jesus were also present at his death, looking on from a distance.

from Mark, chapter 15, verses 21–40

Above
Wine mixed with myrrh.

Crucifixion

Crucifixion was a form of execution often used on slaves, but never on Roman citizens. The Romans crucified criminals at the side of a road, so that people could see them and be warned. The traditional place of Jesus' execution is beside the main road to the coast, just outside the city gate. A placard described their crime; the one for Jesus read, "King of the Jews" to warn travellers on the road what happened to people who made such claims.

At a regular place of execution, upright posts would already be fixed in the ground. The criminal would carry a crosspiece, to which his hands were already fixed, sometimes nailed. The soldiers would then haul up both prisoner and crosspiece on to the upright post. There the prisoner could remain for days, slowly dying. Sometimes, if there were many executions at once, the soldiers would simply nail the prisoners on to trees. The Romans were a tough race, yet even they described crucifixion as "a revolting form of execution".

Simon of Cyrene may have been a member of the large Jewish community in that rich North African town. Pilgrims often came from there for the great festival. Soldiers had a right to pull people in for a task; presumably Simon was passing when Jesus was too weak to carry his crosspiece any further.

The sayings on the cross

The four gospels between them record seven sayings of Jesus on the cross. When Jesus cried out, "My God, my God, why have you forsaken me?" this was the opening line of Psalm 22. The opening words in Aramaic, "*Eloi, Eloi*" made some listeners think that Jesus was calling on the prophet Elijah, who was often called upon to rescue Jews from the power of the Romans.

Overleaf
Jesus was crucified between two criminals.

Below
A Roman centurion.

THE BURIAL IN THE GARDEN

The Jewish authorities did not want the bodies still hanging on the cross on the sabbath day (the Passover sabbath was especially important to them). They asked, therefore, that the prisoners' legs might be broken, so the bodies could be taken away. The soldiers did, indeed, break the legs of the two men crucified with Jesus, but when they came to Jesus, they found that he was already dead. They didn't break his legs, therefore, but one of the soldiers stuck a spear in his side, and blood and water came out immediately. The one telling you this was an eyewitness, and his words are true; he knows he is telling the truth, so you may believe.

Joseph of Arimathaea (who was a secret follower of Jesus because he was scared of the Jewish authorities) obtained Pilate's permission to take away Jesus' body.

Nicodemus (who had earlier visited Jesus one night) brought about 30 kilos of spices, a mixture of myrrh and aloes. They took Jesus' body, and wrapped it with the spices in linen cloths, as is the Jewish custom for a burial. Near the place of crucifixion there was a garden, and in the garden was a brand-new tomb – no bodies had ever been laid in it. They put Jesus in this nearby tomb, because it was the day before the sabbath.

from John, chapter 19, verses 31–42

Jesus' body was carried down the steps of the tomb, a little room cut into the rock.

Hastening death

At a crucifixion, the weight of the body, hanging from the arms, pulled down on the lungs, making it difficult to breathe. But the feet were also nailed, which meant that a strong man could go on taking breaths by pushing himself up on his nailed feet. Even a strong man, however, would eventually die of slow suffocation and loss of blood. Breaking the prisoner's legs would mean that he could no longer pull himself up to breathe, and so died quickly.

Burial

Whereas the Romans often left bodies hanging on the cross for months, the Jews believed that the body of a criminal hung on a tree was cursed by God. If left, it would bring a curse on the whole land. So the Jews normally asked permission of the Romans to bury the bodies of executed criminals. In this case the Passover sabbath was a very holy day. It was necessary, therefore, to end the execution quickly. Nicodemus was a Pharisee, and would want to be particularly careful that the sabbath should not be made unclean.

Executed criminals were normally buried in a public grave owned by the city council. Most Jewish tombs in Jerusalem were cut into the rock. A short flight of steps led down to a small underground chamber, about three metres square. Into the walls of this chamber were cut several little galleries, just long enough to hold a body. The body was wrapped in a cloth with sweet-smelling spices. It was placed in one of these galleries, and the approach-tunnel was then blocked with a large stone. When the body had decomposed, the bones were placed in a casket.

Joseph of Arimathaea was a member of the council of Jewish elders known as the Sanhedrin. It has been suggested that he was in charge of the criminals' grave. However, the accounts stress that this grave was a fresh one, and no one had yet been buried in it. The huge quantity of spices brought by Nicodemus shows his generosity and his personal involvement.

Above
Preparations for anointing the body.

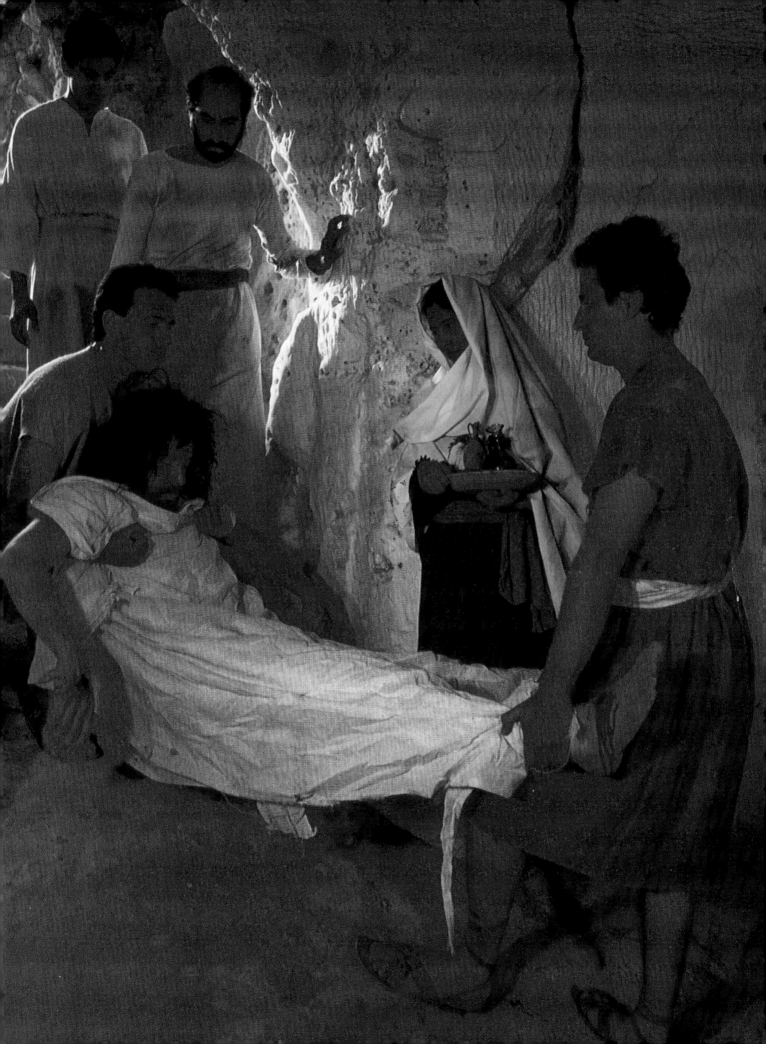

JESUS APPEARS TO MARY

Early Sunday morning, while it was still dark, Mary of Magdala went to the tomb. When she saw that the stone had been taken away from the entrance to the tomb, she ran to Simon Peter and the other disciple (the disciple who was Jesus' close friend) and said to them, "They have taken the Lord out of the tomb, and we don't know where they have put him." Peter and the other disciple went to the tomb – they both ran, but the other disciple was faster, and got there first. Crouching to look into the tomb, he saw the linen cloths, but he did not go in. Then Peter arrived. He went into the tomb, and saw the cloths lying there, and the napkin which had been wrapped around the head lying folded by itself. The other disciple followed him into the tomb. He saw and believed. (They did not yet understand what it said in the Scriptures, that he would rise from the dead.) So the two disciples went away.

Mary, left alone, stood weeping near the tomb. She turned round and saw Jesus, though at first she didn't know it was him. Jesus said to her, "Dear lady, why are you crying?" She thought he was the gardener. "Sir, if you have moved the body, tell me where you have put it and I will take it away," she said.

Jesus said to her, "Mary!" By now she was looking straight at him, and she said to him in Aramaic, "*Rabboni!*" (meaning "Teacher"). Jesus told her, "Don't touch me – I've not yet gone up to my Father. But go to my brothers and tell them that I am returning to the One who is my Father and your Father, even my God and your God." So Mary went and told the disciples that she had seen the Lord, and what he had said to her.

Mary of Magdala returned to the tomb and found the stone covering the entrance had been rolled away.

from John, chapter 20, verses 1–18

The empty tomb

Each of the four gospels has a story of the tomb of Jesus being found empty. Was his body stolen? The Gospel of Matthew says the guards reported that the disciples stole the body while they were asleep; the chief priests bribed them to tell this improbable story.

The early Christians were convinced that Christ was alive and had appeared to them alive. Some twenty years later, the apostle Paul, writing to his Christian friends at Corinth, reminds them of the basic message they had all learnt by heart: *Christ appeared to Peter and later to the Twelve; next he appeared to more than 500 of the brothers at the same time.* They all felt that Christ was not someone dead and gone, someone of the past, but was still among them and active in them. Not only was he their inspiration and their strength: for a time he had been bodily among them. He could appear in a locked room and disappear again. But he was not a ghost, for he could eat and be touched.

It was a Jewish custom to visit the graves of friends. Three days after the crucifixion some women had gone to visit the tomb; they came back, terrified, to tell the men they had received a heavenly message that Jesus was alive and in Galilee. One of them, Mary of Magdala, even claimed that she had caught a glimpse of Jesus standing and moving in the garden. Then they remembered that Jesus had said that he would be raised from the dead.

For centuries Jews had believed that the dead somehow continued to live in God's hands. But this was something new: Jesus was face to face with God, but also active among his followers on earth.

Above
The burial cloths.

THE STRANGER ON THE ROAD TO EMMAUS

Two disciples were going to a village called Emmaus, about eleven kilometres out of Jerusalem. They were chatting about all the things that had happened. Jesus approached and walked with them, though they didn't recognize him.

Jesus said, "What are you talking about? Why are you so upset?" One of them, who was called Cleopas, answered, "You must be the only visitor to Jerusalem who hasn't heard what's happened these last few days!" They told him everything that had happened to Jesus. "We had hoped that he was the one who would save Israel," they said, sighing.

"How brainless you are. How slow you have been to understand the prophecies in the Scriptures. The Christ had to suffer these things, and enter heaven," Jesus told them. Starting with Moses and the prophets, he explained to them how all the Scriptures pointed to Jesus.

They drew near to Emmaus. Jesus seemed to be intending to go further, but they urged him to stay, saying, "It's evening. The day is already over." So he went into the house with them. As he lay at the table with them, he took the loaf of bread, gave thanks to God, broke it and gave it to them. Suddenly they saw who it was, and realized it was Jesus – and then he was gone.

from Luke, chapter 24, verses 13–31

Below

When Jesus took the bread, blessed and broke it, his companions immediately recognized him.

The stranger

Why didn't they recognize him? Perhaps it was already getting dark? However, darkness falls very quickly in Palestine; the sun sets over the Mediterranean in about five minutes, and it is pitch dark twenty minutes later. Perhaps he was wrapped up to protect himself against the dust of the journey. But in all the stories of appearances of the risen Jesus, the disciples have some difficulty in recognizing him. He somehow looked different, and yet was found to be the same.

How the Bible pointed to Jesus

The disappointment of Jesus' death must have been terrible. He had been the great leader, a man with a wonderful, magnetic personality. People would follow him anywhere, drop everything at a moment's notice. Some of them expected him to be the King who would make Israel a great people again. Yet it all ended in the execution of a criminal, deserted by his friends and teased by his enemies as he hung dying, alone except for two criminals in the same disgrace.

The stranger explained it through the Scriptures. For the Jews the Scriptures were the record of how God had treated his people, Israel, how he had looked after them through all the crises of their history.

Breaking bread

Very soon, Christians began to gather for a meal in memory of Jesus' Last Supper with his disciples, to celebrate his work in gratitude. The central act of the meal was always "breaking bread" as he had himself done at the Last Supper. At a normal meal, the senior person present broke the loaf of bread and passed it round to the others. When Jesus joined the two travellers as their guest, they would never expect him to take on this task. And that was how they knew who he was; he was the host and they were his friends.

Cleopas and his companion travelling to Emmaus were joined by a stranger.

Overleaf

The disciples found their nets filled with fish.

212

THE GREAT CATCH OF FISH

Right
Fish cooked on a fire.

Simon Peter, Thomas the Twin, Nathanael of Cana in Galilee, James and John, and two other disciples were together by the Sea of Galilee. Simon Peter said to them, "I'm off to fish!" and they said, "We'll come with you." They were in the boat all night, but caught nothing. At dawn, Jesus stood on the shore (though they did not realize it was him). He shouted, "Have you caught any fish, lads?" "No," they answered. "Throw in the net to the starboard side and you'll get some," said Jesus.

When they did so, they caught so many fish that they could not pull the net back in. The disciple who was Jesus' close friend said, "It is the Lord." At this, Peter put on his tunic (he had stripped off to work) and jumped into the water. The other disciples sailed towards the beach – they were only about 100 metres from land. They saw that Jesus had built a small charcoal fire. A small fish was cooking, and there was some bread. Simon Peter got into the boat and dragged the net ashore. Although they had caught 153 fish, the net hadn't broken. "Come and have breakfast," Jesus said to them.

After they had eaten breakfast, Jesus said to Simon Peter, "Simon, son of John, do you love me more than these?" Peter said, "Yes, Lord, you know I'm your friend." "Feed my lambs," said Jesus. He said a second time, "Simon, son of John, do you love me?" Peter said, "Yes, Lord, you know I'm your friend." "Look after my sheep," said Jesus. Then Jesus asked a third time, "Simon, son of John, are you my friend?" Peter was upset that Jesus asked him this a third time. He said, "Lord, you know everything. You know I'm your friend." Jesus said, "Feed my sheep. Amen, amen, I say to you, when you were young you went wherever you wanted. When you get old you will be chained and taken where you don't want to go." (He was telling Peter the way he would die.) Then Jesus told him, "Just follow me!"

from John, chapter 21, verses 2–12, 15–19

Jesus forgives Peter

At Jesus' Last Supper, Peter had sworn loyalty till death, but then, scared by a little girl, he had three times sworn he didn't even know Jesus. Now Jesus insists that he must three times declare his love and loyalty. The story must have been told among the early Christians to encourage others who failed.

A fishing-harbor

An old tradition attaches this scene to a quiet little inlet on the north shore of the Sea of Galilee. There the square stones of an ancient Roman harbor are still visible on the edge of the water. A few metres away some warm springs flow into the lake.

THE ACTS OF THE APOSTLES

After his death Jesus showed himself to his disciples for a period of forty days. He gave them proof beyond doubt that he had risen from the dead, and told them more about the kingdom of God. After he left them for the last time the disciples returned to Jerusalem. They went into the city and went up into an upper room. Peter and John were there, with James and Andrew, Philip and Thomas, Bartholomew and Matthew, James the son of Alphaeus, Simon the Zealot and Judas the brother of James.

They spent all their time united in prayer, together with the women, Mary the mother of Jesus and his brothers. In those days, Peter took the lead among the brethren (about 120 people were gathered there).

from Acts, chapter 1, verses 3, 12–15

The Book of Acts

This book describes the spread of Christianity from Jerusalem in ever wider circles, first to the rest of Judaea, then to Asia Minor (now called Turkey), then to Greece, and finally to Rome. It is anonymous, but scholars agree that it was written by Luke. It has the same way of putting things as the Gospel of Luke, and the same interests: both show that Jesus came to save all people, not only the Jews; both give a special place to the Spirit of God which guides the Christian community.

The followers of Jesus

According to Luke, the risen Jesus came to the disciples during forty days. He was preparing them for their mission. (The number forty is often associated in the Bible with times of preparation: the Israelites were forty years in the desert, Elijah was forty days preparing for his mission, Jesus was tested in the desert for forty days and nights.) After that, Jesus left them and was seen no more. The little group stayed shut away, huddled in their upper room.

Both Luke's books stress the importance of women in Jesus' group, and especially his mother, Mary. (It is Luke's gospel which gives us the story of the angel's message to Mary and of the birth at Bethlehem.) The Jews especially treasured family values, and the mother was a very important figure. But the Roman women could hold more open and public positions, and as Jesus' followers spread into this world, women played a more important part, sometimes as the hostess and patron of a Christian group meeting in her house, sometimes perhaps even presiding over a group.

The brothers of Jesus

The "brothers of Jesus" are mentioned here. In Palestine the word "brothers" signified not merely children of the same parents but any close male relations, cousins as well as brothers. Whether Jesus had any brothers and sisters has often been questioned. From early times the Christian tradition has held that Mary had no other children but Jesus. So these "brothers" would in fact be cousins. Recently, however, some have held that, with the Jewish emphasis on family life, it would be strange to have one child only: a large family was normal among the Jews in those days, and many people think that a young couple like Mary and Joseph must have had other children.

Below
Peter and the other disciples started to spread the gospel amongst the poor.

217

THE DAY OF PENTECOST

On the day of Pentecost, they were all together in the same place. Suddenly a noise like rushing wind came from heaven; it filled the whole house. Small flames flickered amongst them like fire, resting on each one. They were all filled with the Holy Spirit, and started to speak in languages as the Holy Spirit enabled them.

Many godly Jews from all over the world were living in Jerusalem. All the noise attracted great crowds of people, who were puzzled because each could hear an apostle speaking his language. They were astonished and said, "Look at these Galileans speaking all those different languages." Others laughed at the apostles and said, "They've had too much sweet wine."

Then Peter stood up amongst the Eleven and shouted, "Listen to what I say! These men are not drunk, as you claim – it's only nine o'clock in the morning! What you are seeing are words of the prophet Joel coming true 'In the last days, says God, I will pour out my Spirit on all flesh.' "

Peter preached and concluded, "The whole nation of Israel must realize that God made Jesus – whom you crucified – both Lord and Christ!"

When they heard this, the crowds were very worried and said to Peter and the other apostles, "Brothers, what can we do?" Peter said, "You must change your ways. Each one of you must be baptized in the name of Jesus Christ. Your sins will be forgiven, and you will receive the gift of the Holy Spirit." Many of the crowd accepted what he said, and were baptized; that day about 3000 people became believers.

from Acts, chapter 2, verses 1–17, 36–41

The festival of Pentecost

In ancient Israel the Feast of Pentecost was a harvest festival. It was one of the three great pilgrimage feasts, when large numbers of Jews used to come to Jerusalem.

Later it became the day when Jews celebrated the time when God gave Moses the Law on Mount Sinai. There was a legend that on that day the Spirit of God came down on seventy Jewish heads of families in the form of fire. The Jews thought that there were just seventy nations of the world, and saw this as a sign that the Jewish Law was to spread like a fire to all nations of the world.

Speaking in tongues

Luke is probably thinking of the "speaking in tongues" which happened frequently in the early Christian gatherings. People used strange languages to praise God; these were meaningless unless someone else could interpret them.

In modern times this same "speaking in tongues" is sometimes used in Christian prayer gatherings. A "Pentecostal" Church has grown up where it is a feature of worship. In other Churches, too, people are called "charismatics" (from the Greek word meaning "gift") who use gifts of the Spirit, such as the power to heal.

One day, Peter and John were going to the Temple. It was three o'clock in the afternoon – the time for the daily prayer service. As they arrived, they met a man who had been lame all his life. He was being carried (as he was every day) to be put by the Beautiful Gate, where he begged money from people on their way into the Temple. When he saw Peter and John going in, he asked them to give him something. Peter looked intently at him. With John standing beside him, he said, "Look at us!"

The man gave them his full attention, for he thought he was going to get something. Peter, however, said, "I don't have any silver or gold, but I'll give you what I do have; in the name of Jesus Christ of Nazareth, rise up and walk!" Taking the man by the right hand, Peter pulled him up on to his feet. The man's feet and ankles became strong. He jumped up and went into the Temple with them, walking and leaping, and praising God.

Everybody saw him walking and praising God. They knew he was the man who sat begging at the Beautiful Gate of the Temple, and they were filled with surprise and amazement at what had happened.

from Acts, chapter 3, verses 1–10

Sharing

Luke tells us that sharing was the mark of the first Christian community in Jerusalem. They prayed together. They shared their meals and their possessions. They pooled the money from the sale of their lands, and waited for Jesus to come again.

The first Christians believed that they were already in the last stage of the world's history, and expected the end to come in their own lifetime. So they did not believe there was any need to plan for the future. They pictured the last coming of Jesus as a Roman triumphal procession. In Rome, after a great victory, the general led a wild, rejoicing procession of his army through the streets, to offer the spoils of victory to their gods in the chief temple of the city. The Christians imagined that Christ would come and lead them in such a procession, finally offering to God the Kingdom he had won. In his letters Paul had to calm his converts down. He insisted that no one could tell when all this would happen. They still needed to carry on working. Christ's triumphal procession would not happen in the immediate future.

Christians and the Temple

At first the Christians were not separate from other Jews. They continued to worship in the Temple, and saw themselves as one branch within Judaism. They believed that the Jewish Scriptures themselves pointed to Jesus, and that he fulfilled all the hopes of the Jews. Those who accepted Jesus as Messiah formed a special group within Judaism. Within a few years someone invented for these people the nickname "Christian" (*Christ* is Greek for the Hebrew word *Messiah*).

From the beginning, however, the Temple authorities forbade Jesus' disciples to teach that Jesus was the Christ. Twice the apostles were imprisoned and once they were flogged before they were released. Later Paul also was flogged several times, and describes how his flogging went right up to the legal limit of punishment. The Law allowed forty strokes of the whip, but the rabbis limited it to thirty-nine – to avoid the Law being broken in case of a miscount.

Below
Lydia, a seller of purple cloth. She was a friend to the disciples.

As the number of disciples grew, the Greek-speaking believers murmured against the Jewish believers. They claimed that their widows were not getting a fair share of the daily food hand-outs. The twelve apostles called them all together and said, "It is not right that we neglect the word of God to become food-waiters! Choose seven respected men, who are wise and full of the Holy Spirit, to look after this matter. We will concentrate on prayer and preaching."

Seven Greeks were appointed and the apostles laid hands on them. One, Stephen, was especially respected.

from Acts, chapter 6, verses 1–5

Left
The Greek disciples complained that they were disregarded by the Jewish disciples. It was decided that the Greeks would choose their own representatives.

The *Diakonia*

The Jews had a system of poor relief, involving a weekly hand-out of food. A number of old people came to live in Jerusalem towards the end of their lives: they wanted to die in the Holy City. Probably quite a lot of them needed help – a sort of ancient welfare service. The early Church increased this service to a daily one, called the *Diakonia*. Luke tells how seven respected people in the community were appointed to be in charge of this. But they also preached and baptized and witnessed to Jesus. It is striking that they all have Greek names. So some scholars have suggested that eleven of the original disciples and a twelfth elected following Judas' death remained the leaders of the Hebrew-speaking Christians and the Seven were really the leaders of those who spoke Greek. This would show two Christian communities in Jerusalem, one beside the other. The Bible account suggests that in fact the two groups were quarrelling and wanted to remain separate.

Final separation

In AD 66 the Jews rebelled against Rome. The Roman armies besieged Jerusalem for four years. Anyone who escaped from Jerusalem was caught, nailed up to the trees of the Mount of Olives opposite Jerusalem, and left to die within sight of the walls of the city. Finally the Romans captured Jerusalem and pulled down the Temple.

In the sad time that followed, the Jews began to rebuild their community, but by now they regarded the Christians as a quite separate group.

The Jews who did not accept the preaching of the apostles were especially hostile to the Greek-speaking followers of Jesus. These were the first to be persecuted. In any case, gradually opposition between the Jesus-group and the rest of the Jews became more violent. Non-Christian Jews could not accept the Christian view that Jesus had been God's Son, that he was still alive and active.

The Christians who had been in Jerusalem fled to Pella on the other side of the Jordan, and made their center there.

In AD 132 another rebellion of the Jews broke out and after this Jerusalem was changed into a totally Roman city, called Aelia Capitolina. No Jews were allowed to live in any part of Judaea any more.

STEPHEN, THE FIRST MARTYR

Stephen, full of grace and power, did great wonders and signs among the people. Some of the men who belonged to the Synagogue of the Freedmen (as it was called) argued with Stephen, but they could not stand up to the wisdom and the Spirit with which he spoke. So they whipped up the people, the Jewish leaders and the scribes, against Stephen. They seized him and took him before the Sanhedrin. They produced false witnesses who lied, "This man is always criticizing the Temple and the Law."

After a long speech describing Jewish history Stephen said, "You stubborn, godless men. You have always opposed the Holy Spirit. Name one of the prophets your ancestors didn't persecute! Now you have betrayed and murdered the Holy One they prophesied about. You were given God's Law by heavenly messengers – but you have never kept it."

The members of the Sanhedrin became so angry they ground their teeth at him. Stephen, however, was filled with the Holy Spirit and had a vision of God's glory. "Look! I can see into heaven, and there I see Jesus standing at God's right hand!" he said. At this, they shouted out, stuck their fingers in their ears and charged at him. Then they cast him out of the city and stoned him to death. Yet even as he was being stoned, Stephen prayed, "Lord, receive my spirit!" He knelt down and shouted out, "Lord, don't hold this sin against them." Then he died. The witnesses left their cloaks at the feet of a young man named Saul.

Stephen's killing by stoning was encouraged by Jewish officials.

from Acts, chapters 6–7

Death by stoning

Later Jewish Law lays down exactly how stoning should be carried out. The convicted man is bound hand and foot. The first witness pushes him over a cliff at least four metres high, so that he falls on his head and breaks his neck. The second witness is waiting to drop a large rock on the convict, in case he is not dead. Then the rest of the crowd add their own stones. But, as the Jews at this time had no right to execute anyone, this may not have been an official execution. Perhaps a mob just dragged Stephen out and killed him.

Above
Stephen.

Stephen was the first "martyr"; by his death he witnessed (in Greek *martyr*) his loyalty to Christ. As Luke tells this story, he is careful to stress the parallels between Stephen's death and that of Jesus. Both spoke against the Temple, both forgave their killers, and both gave themselves into God's hands as they died.

Saul becomes Paul

The Saul mentioned here as a witness against Stephen later becomes Paul the apostle of Christ. In the Greek world Jews often had two names, one for the Greeks and one for the Jews. Saul was the name originally borne by the first king of Israel. Paul was a name common in Turkey, where this Paul was born at Tarsus. The Roman general Aemilius Paullus gave many people in this area Roman citizenship, probably for helping his military operations there. The families would take the name of the general who gave them their citizenship. To be a citizen of Rome was to be especially privileged.

PHILIP AND THE ETHIOPIAN

A messenger of the Lord said to Philip, one of the "deacons", "Get up, take the desert road from Jerusalem to Gaza, and head south." So Philip went, and as he travelled, he suddenly saw an Ethiopian. This man was a eunuch, the minister of the Candace – the Queen of Ethiopia. He had gone to Jerusalem to worship and was on his way home. As he sat in the chariot, he was reading the Scriptures.

The Holy Spirit said to Philip, "Go to that chariot and run beside it." As he ran along, Philip heard the man reading from the prophecies of Isaiah. "Do you understand it?" he said. "How can I, unless someone explains it?" said the man, and he asked Philip to travel with him in the chariot.

Now the Ethiopian was reading this passage of the Scriptures: "He was like a sheep taken to be slaughtered. Like a lamb, who cannot speak to the shearer, he refused to speak. He was humiliated, and was denied a fair trial." The man asked Philip, "Who is Isaiah talking about, himself or someone else?" At this, starting with that passage of Scripture, Philip explained to him the good news of Jesus. They had reached a small pool by the wayside. The man said, "Look! Water! What is there to stop me being baptized now?" He ordered the chariot to stop. They both went down into the water, and Philip baptized him.

Below
Scrolls were read.

from Acts, chapter 8, verses 26–38

The eunuch

A eunuch means a man who is unable to father children because he has been castrated (this means his testicles have been removed). This operation was performed on young boys (and perhaps prisoners of war). Eastern rulers especially chose young boys to be made eunuchs so that when they were old enough they could use such men as state officials and supervisors of the harem, the royal women's living area. As they were incapable of fathering children, there was no danger they would set up a rival royal dynasty to the king. People often considered them figures of fun, a sort of half-man, so they would need royal protection and therefore their loyalty could be counted on by the king or queen.

According to Jewish Law eunuchs could not become full Jews, so at most this man must have been a "God-fearer", someone who honored God and was attached to the Jewish way of life. This man was an Ethiopian, living well beyond what was then considered civilization, in the area now known as the Sudan. He would have been despised for that reason too. So the first non-Jew to be welcomed into Christianity was from the lowest of the low: a half-man, servant of a woman, from a country well beyond civilization.

Reading the Scriptures

Philip would hear the reading because in those days, and long afterwards, reading was always done aloud. (Four hundred years later, Augustine was amazed to see Ambrose, Bishop of Milan, reading a book without making any sound.) So Philip would have heard the eunuch reading the passage of Isaiah. Although Isaiah's prophecy referred directly to the suffering of a servant of the Lord at the time of the exile of the Jews in Babylon, Philip explained to the eunuch that it also referred to Jesus and his suffering.

Philip and the Ethiopian went down to the water and Philip baptized him.

226

PAUL ON THE ROAD TO DAMASCUS

Saul continued to utter threats and murder against the Lord's disciples. He persuaded the high priest to write to the leaders of the synagogues in Damascus. He wanted to search out the believers there – men and women – and bring them back in chains to Jerusalem.

On the way to Damascus, a light from heaven suddenly flashed round him. He fell to the ground. Then he heard a voice which said, "Saul, Saul, why are you persecuting me?" He said, "Lord, who are you?" The Lord said, "I am Jesus, whom you are persecuting. Get up and go into the city, where you will be told what to do." The men with Saul were speechless. They heard the voice, but could not see anyone. Saul stood up, but he had been blinded. They led him by the hand to Damascus. For three days he was unable to see, and did not eat or drink.

In Damascus lived a disciple named Ananias. The Lord told him in a vision, "Go to Straight Street, to the house of Judas. Ask for a man named Saul, who is praying there. He has had a vision, and is expecting a man named Ananias to go and lay hands on him, so he can regain his sight." Ananias answered, "Lord, I've heard about this man. He has done many evil things to the saints in Jerusalem, and he has the high priest's authority to arrest all those who believe in your Name." But the Lord said to him, "Go! He is my chosen vessel, and he will carry my Name to all nations."

Ananias went in and laid hands on Saul. Immediately something like scales fell from Saul's eyes, and he got his sight back. He got up and was baptized, then he ate and got his strength back.

from Acts, chapter 9, verses 1–19

Left
Saul got up from the ground. Although his eyes were open he could not see.

Ananias went to Straight Street and found the house of Judas.

The conversion of Paul

This event was so important that Luke gives the story three times at different points in his gospel. Once he tells the story, and twice he shows Paul telling his own story. From this point Saul is known by his new name 'Paul'. Luke wants to stress how startling the conversion was, and how important was Paul's mission in the spread of Christianity.

The vision

No one can know exactly what happened on the road to Damascus. Paul describes his experience of Christ in terms of a voice from heaven and a blinding light, which left him blind for three days. The voice made him realize that Christ was present in the very people he was persecuting. He realized that he was being called to serve Christ, in the same way as the great figures of the Bible, such as Abraham and Moses, had been called.

Through the strength of that experience Paul came to work as hard for Christ and his followers as he had previously worked against them. His energetic journeying and preaching resulted in Christian communities being set up in Turkey, then in Greece, and possibly as far west as Spain. He wrote letters to help and guide them, and sometimes to correct them fiercely.

CORNELIUS

In Caesarea lived a centurion of the Italian Cohort named Cornelius. He was very religious; he and all his household feared God. He gave to the poor and spent a lot of time praying to God. About three o'clock in the afternoon, he had a vision. A messenger of God said to him, "Cornelius, send men to Joppa. Invite a man called Simon Peter to come to you. He is staying at the house of Simon the Tanner, who lives by the sea."

Next day, about noon, Peter had gone up on the roof to pray. He became hungry. While he was waiting for the food to be prepared, he had a vision. Something like a huge sheet, lowered by its four corners, came down from heaven. In it were all kinds of animals, reptiles and birds. He heard a voice which said, "Get up, Peter. Kill and eat." Peter replied, "Certainly not, Lord! I've never eaten anything unholy or unclean." Then he heard the voice a second time. "Do not call unholy what God has purified."

Cornelius' messengers arrived, and Peter went to Caesarea. He went into Cornelius' house, where he found many people gathered. He said to them, "You know it is against the Jewish Law for a Jew to visit a foreigner, but God has shown me in a vision not to call anybody unholy or unclean. I realize now that God treats everybody the same. He loves those who fear him and do good works, whatever their race."

Peter preached to them, telling them about Jesus Christ. While he was speaking, the Holy Spirit fell on all the listeners. The Jewish believers were astonished, for they heard the Gentiles speaking in tongues and glorifying God. Peter said, "Will anyone forbid these people, who have received the Holy Spirit, to be baptized?"

from Acts, chapter 10, verses 1–47

The capital of Roman Palestine

Caesarea was built by King Herod, and named in honor of his friend and patron, Augustus Caesar. It was the greatest port of the eastern Mediterranean, a fine protected harbour, with grand buildings along the waterfront, a large theatre and a stone aqueduct bringing a continuous flow of fresh water from the hills thirty two kilometres away. It was the residence of the Roman governor of Palestine and his garrison. There is an inscription in the theatre which says that Pontius Pilate (who gave the order to execute Jesus) repaired it when he was governor. Besides the official temples of the Roman gods like Jupiter, there was also a Temple of Mithras, a sun-god and a god of courage. It had a special window, through which the sun shone on the altar at noon of midsummer's day.

The centurion Cornelius

Cornelius was named after the general Cornelius Sulla. Over a century earlier, Cornelius Sulla had freed many slaves, who all took his name for their families. He was obviously more sympathetic to the Jewish religion than most Romans, but no Roman had yet become a Christian. Peter needed a great deal of persuading to accept him as a Christian! A Jew could not go into the house of a non-Jew, or touch his food or possessions – they were considered unclean. First, however, came the vision of the unclean animals in the sheet, and the voice which told Peter that all God's creatures are good. Then the Holy Spirit came upon the Roman and his household, just as it had come upon the apostles at Pentecost. After the Holy Spirit had come upon them, Peter could hardly refuse to accept them. But he later had a great deal of trouble explaining his action to the other leaders of the Church in Jerusalem. Many of them thought that only Jews could become Christians, but this was a decisive step in the spread of Christianity to all nations.

Peter prayed on the roof of the house belonging to Simon the tanner.

THE MISSION TO SPREAD THE GOSPEL

At Antioch the Holy Spirit said, "Set apart for me Barnabas and Paul, so they can do the work I called them to." Having fasted and prayed, they laid their hands on them, and sent them out.

from Acts, chapter 13, verses 1–3

At Lystra

In Lystra they were heard by a man who had been lame from birth; he had never walked, because he was crippled in his feet. When Paul saw that the man believed he could be healed, he looked intently at him and said loudly, "Get up on to your feet!" The man jumped up and started walking about.

When they saw this, the crowds said (in Lycaonian), "The gods have come down to us in the form of men!" They decided that Barnabas was Zeus and that Paul was Hermes (because he did the talking). The local priest of Zeus, whose temple was near by, brought bulls and garlands to the city gates. It was with the greatest difficulty that Paul and Barnabas prevented the crowds from offering a sacrifice to them.

from Acts, chapter 14, verses 8–18

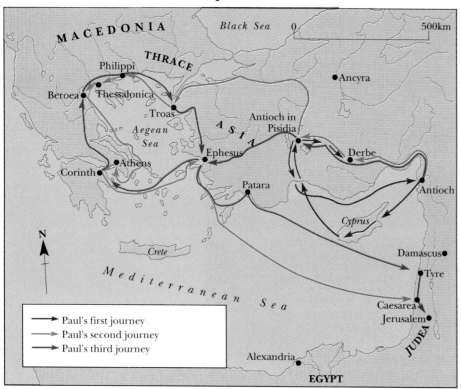

Paul's first journey
Paul's second journey
Paul's third journey

Paul the Healer

Luke shows by this narrative that the disciples of Jesus carried on his work. They spread the Good News of the Kingdom of God by their words, and also by their deeds, healing the sick and the lame, just as Jesus had done.

Paul's journeys

The network of Roman roads throughout the Empire made journeying easier than at any time till a hundred years ago. They were great roads, like a two-metre-wide wall sunk into the ground and topped with paving-stones. They ran straight, sometimes for hundreds of miles. Transport across the sea was also easy, and it seems to have been possible for travellers to hitch a lift on a ship.

Above
Paul's first three journeys took about eighteen years and covered most of the area we call Turkey, and part of Greece.

Antioch sends its messengers

Antioch was one of the greatest cities in the world, with a population of half a million, on the main trade route from India to Rome. It had a large Jewish community, and Barnabas was sent from Jerusalem to be head of the flourishing Christian community. It was at Antioch that they were first called "Christians". The community appointed Barnabas and Paul as their two representatives to spread the message. On their first journey, Barnabas was the leader and champion of Paul. Afterwards Paul set out alone, and Barnabas disappears from the scene.

Paul had the additional advantage of the little Jewish communities in each town – a natural base where he would be made welcome. But again and again things turned sour when Paul began to teach about Jesus. The pattern repeated itself at each stage, first in Turkey, then in Greece and finally at Rome: Paul tried to bring the Jews to accept Jesus. They refused and turned against Paul. So Paul was sadly forced to turn to non-Jews.

Paul wrote:

Difficulties and dangers

I have frequently been in prison. Five times I received thirty-nine lashes from the Jews. Three times I was beaten with rods. Once I was stoned. Three times I was shipwrecked.

On my journeys I have been in danger from rivers, from robbers, from my own people, from foreigners – danger in the city, in the desert, at sea, among false friends, in labor and hardship, in all-night prayer vigils, in hunger and thirst, in frequent fasting, in cold and exposure.

2 Corinthians, chapter 11, verses 23–27

The travel diary

The source of information for Paul's journeys is the Book of Acts and Paul's own letters to his friends and the communities he looked after. He sent his best wishes to friends, but did not spend much time on travel news. For this need to rely on Luke's Acts of the Apostles. This is remarkably accurate on details. Every city had a different system of government: Philippi was a Roman military colony, governed by "generals". Thessalonica was a "free city" governed by city councillors.

Luke got all these political details right.

At Troas

Paul and Timothy travelled through Galatia. They came down to Troas. That night Paul had a dream in which he saw a Macedonian begging, "Come over to Macedonia and help us!" They immediately got ready to go to Macedonia. They felt that God had called them to tell the Macedonians the Good News. They left by ship and sailed to Greece.
from Acts, chapter 16, verses 6–11

Crossing to Greece

From the Plains of Troy (called "Troas" in Paul's day) they could look across the kilometre or so of sea to Greece, the northern province of Macedonia. And that was how the momentous step was taken of bringing the Good News of Jesus to Europe.

It is not easy to give an exact date for Paul's journeys. In each place the year was called after the chief ruler – "during the consulship of . . .". We have one invaluable clue, the name "Gallio": the Jews of Corinth presented Paul for trial before the proconsul Gallio. An inscription on stone tells us that Gallio was governor in Corinth in early AD 52 (he ran off home when it got hot, afraid that the heat at Corinth would make him ill).

Below
In about AD 58 Paul undertook what is thought to be his final journey to Rome.

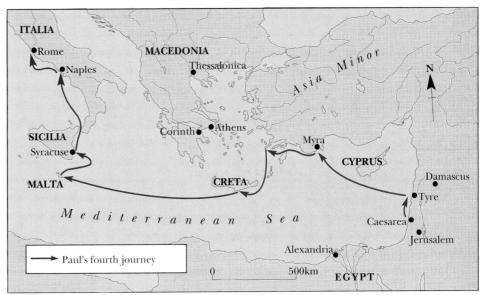

PAUL IN ATHENS

In Athens Paul argued in the synagogue with the Jews and the God-fearers, and every day in the market-place with the passers-by. He also met some of the Stoic and Epicurean philosophers, but they said, "What is this chatterer talking about?" Eventually, they took him to the Areopagus, saying, "Tell us this new teaching. You say strange things; we want to know what they mean." (All Athenians are obsessed to know the latest ideas.)

Paul stood up and said, "Athenians, I see you are very religious, for on my way I saw all your gods – and also an altar with the inscription, 'To an unknown god'. I'll tell you about that God, the one you worship without knowing. This God, who made the world and everything in it, the Lord of heaven and earth, does not live in temples built by man. He doesn't need help from anyone. He has given us life, breath and all we have. As your own poets have written, 'We also are his children.'

"Now, if we really are God's children, we should no longer imagine God as a statue. God is prepared to overlook our ignorance, but he now commands all people, everywhere, to change their ways. God has set a day when all people will be judged by his chosen one – and the proof of this is that he raised him from the dead." When they heard about the resurrection of the dead, some laughed at him. Others said, "We must hear more about this." So Paul left them. Some men and women, however, joined him.

from Acts, chapter 17, verses 17–34

The city of learning

For more than 500 years Athens had been the intellectual capital of the world. Students from all over the world attended its university.

Paul worked his speech to them very cleverly. In any great public place there were statues and little altars in honor of the many gods. In case one of the gods got offended by being left out, there would be one altar "to an unknown god". Paul took this altar as his starting point. Then he spoke to each of the main philosophical schools. Philosophers in the university of Athens were divided into two "schools", called Epicureans and Stoics. The Epicureans thought the gods didn't interfere with the world, but lived happily in heaven; they would nod enthusiastically when Paul said, "He doesn't need help from anyone." He actually quoted a poet of the Stoics, to support his argument that God is our Father.

It was when Paul got to the resurrection of Jesus from the dead that the trouble started. His proclamation that Jesus rose was too much for them. Paul was upset by his failure at Athens, and afterwards resolved to preach rather than argue points of philosophy.

The speeches in *Acts*

There are over 130 speeches in Acts. If a Greek historian did not know what a person actually said, he wrote down what that person *should* or *might* have said. Some scholars have claimed that Luke did the same, and put in standard sermons for the various occasions. But a closer look shows that there is quite a difference between the speeches of Peter, Paul and James. Paul's speeches in Acts stress many of the points he stresses in his letters, further testifying to their authenticity.

Paul stood up in front of the Areopagus and debated with the Athenians.

PAUL AT EPHESUS

In Ephesus, Paul spent three months teaching in the Jewish synagogue, but the Jews refused to believe. So Paul and his followers left them. For two years, Paul held discussions every day in the lecture hall of Tyrannus.

About this time a riot took place in Ephesus because of The Way [Christianity]. Local workmen had made large profits by making little silver shrines of the goddess Artemis. A silversmith called Demetrius gathered them together and said, "Men, you know that we made a good living from this work. You also know that in Ephesus and all over Asia, this Paul is convincing people that statues are not real gods. Not just our work is in danger. There is a chance that people will stop respecting the goddess Artemis (who is worshipped by all the world)." When they heard this, they were furious and shouted, "Great is Artemis of Ephesus." The city was in an uproar. They seized two Macedonians who were travelling with Paul and dragged them to the theatre. Most of them had no idea why they had gathered. For two hours they chanted, "Great is Artemis of Ephesus."

Eventually the town scribe quietened them. He said, "Ephesians! Everyone knows that the city of Ephesus is temple-keeper of the great Artemis, and of the sacred stone that fell from the sky. These things are undeniable. So you must calm down. If you have a complaint, it must be settled in the regular *ekklesia*. We don't want to be accused of having a riot." Then with this he sent them home.

from Acts, chapter 19, verses 8–9, 23–41

Below
A statuette of Artemis.

The great city of Ephesus

Ephesus was the greatest city and the capital of the Roman province of Asia (in modern Turkey). It was at the mouth of a great river, the chief market and port of Asia, with a population of a quarter of a million. Many of its fine marble buildings still stand; one street is built entirely of marble. The Temple of Artemis was one of the seven wonders of the ancient world. Its theatre is set into the side of a hill, and can hold 24,000 spectators. The lecture hall used by Tyrannus for philosophical discussions would have been deserted during the hottest part of the day when Paul was able to hold his own mission there. Like all cities in the Roman Empire, Ephesus kept its own government. The public assembly (the *ekklesia*) met regularly in the theatre.

The city was famous all over the Mediterranean for its shrine of Artemis, the goddess of wild beasts and hunting. At Ephesus she was also thought to be responsible for the fruitfulness of the land and for healthy child-bearing.

Paul and Ephesus

Paul had a great affection for the Ephesians. He visited the city twice, and on this second visit stayed for two years. During some of this time he was probably imprisoned. In spite of these difficulties, he built up a strong Christian community there. After a visit in Corinth and on his way back to Jerusalem, expecting to be taken prisoner, he summoned the elders of the Christian community to a nearby town. There he gave them a long farewell speech. Later, when he was already a prisoner, he wrote them one of his greatest letters.

The silversmiths gathered in the theatre at Ephesus. They shouted furiously against Paul and his teaching.

Right
*The stormy
Mediterranean Sea
in winter.*

Paul went to Jerusalem, where he was arrested. He claimed the right of a Roman citizen to be tried by the emperor and was put on a ship bound for Rome.

By now it was almost winter and dangerous to sail, so Paul advised, "If we continue our voyage we will lose the cargo, the ship and even our lives." However, when a gentle wind began to blow from the south, the men raised the anchor and set off along the coast.

Soon, however, a gale-force wind blew. The sailors threw the cargo overboard and tied thick ropes around the ship so it didn't fall apart. After fourteen days the storm eased.

The sailors did not recognize the coastline, but they now saw a bay with a beach, and decided to run the ship aground there. They cut the anchors and the ropes which held the rudders. Then

they hoisted a foresail and sailed towards the shore. The ship, however, stuck fast on a sandbank. Behind, the waves were pounding it to pieces. The soldiers wanted to kill the prisoners to stop them swimming ashore and escaping, but the centurion – who wanted to save Paul – would not let them. Instead, he ordered all those who could swim to jump overboard and get to land, and everybody else to hold on to planks. When they were all ashore, they learned that the island was called Malta.

from Acts, chapter 27

*When the ship sank
everyone who could
swim jumped
overboard.*

Paul's arrest

Paul was the chief influence in bringing non-Jews to Christianity. This made him highly suspect to Jews, both Christian and non-Christian. In Jerusalem most of the followers of Jesus' teaching (which they called "The Way") were Jews, and saw Jesus' teaching as the fulfilment of Judaism. They were reluctant to allow non-Jews to join the Christian community. Many of them wanted to keep the Jewish restrictions about food, and were not happy to eat with non-Jewish Christians.

One of Paul's assistants in Jerusalem was a Greek called Trophimus. One day, when Paul was in the Temple, a riot broke out because some Jews thought Paul had illegally brought Trophimus into the Temple. Paul was rescued in the nick of time by the Roman guards, who were stationed overlooking the Temple, on the alert for such disturbances. As Paul was a Roman citizen, he had a right to a proper trial, whereas non-citizens could be flogged or even executed by Roman magistrates without a formal trial. (Every Roman citizen carried a passport to prove his citizenship, signed by twelve Roman citizens of his own town; there were penalties for falsifying such a document.)

Paul was transferred to Caesarea in the governor's charge. This may be because the Jews were hostile to him. Two governors successively seem to have been puzzled by his case. Paul defended himself, and showed that he had committed no offence against Jewish Law. Asked if he would stand trial before the Jewish court, Paul realized that he had no hope of a fair trial, appealed his case to the Emperor and was sent to Rome under guard.

Overleaf
*Paul, chained and
under house arrest in
Rome, continued to
preach, and write and
dictate letters.*

So we came to Rome. When the believers there heard we were coming, welcoming parties met us at the Forum of Appius and the Three Inns. When he saw them, Paul thanked God and was encouraged.

When we arrived in Rome, the centurion handed Paul over to the local prefect of the Praetorian Guard, but he allowed Paul to live by himself, guarded by one soldier.

He lived in his own house which he rented, and there he welcomed everyone who visited him. He had complete freedom to proclaim the kingdom of God and to teach about Jesus Christ without hindrance.

from Acts, chapter 28, verses 14–16, 30–31

To Rome

After his difficult journey under guard, Paul was greeted like a triumphant general by welcoming parties from the flourishing Christian community already established in Rome. He had earlier written to them his great Letter to the Romans, the longest of all his letters. At the end of it he sent greetings to twenty-eight people by name and to several families too; so he already knew a number of people. Christianity had obviously already spread rapidly in Rome, probably through traders and others returning from Judaea.

Three Inns was one day's journey from Rome on the Appian Way. By horse-drawn cart 56 kilometres was considered an average day's journey on these good roads (though the Emperor Tiberius once, in a crisis, rode 320 kilometres in 24 hours).

Paul in Rome

In Rome there were no prisons, only a small dungeon for prisoners awaiting execution. Those who had to be kept in custody remained under house arrest (Paul had to pay for his lodgings). He would have been permanently handcuffed to a soldier. This does not seem to have prevented Paul both preaching and writing letters to communities he had founded all over the Roman world. In any case, he dictated most of his letters and often named his co-author, who may have been a sort of secretary. Paul often added a few sentences in his own handwriting at the end of letters he had dictated.

The gospel-writer Luke tells how Paul had a final discussion with the Jews of Rome. Some were convinced and became Christians. Others did not, and Paul again turns from them to non-Jews, as he had done in Turkey and Greece. Paul's Letter to the Romans makes it clear that his failure to convert his own Jewish brothers to Christianity was a great sadness to him.

The end of the story

Once he had settled Paul in Rome, Luke breaks off the story: he had reached his goal in the capital of world empire. Nobody knows for sure what happened to Paul in the chaos that followed the Emperor Nero's appalling persecution of the Christian community in AD 64. In that year there was a great fire in Rome. Nero blamed the Christians and had many of them executed. This was only the first of the great persecutions. Another occurred under the Emperor Domitian in AD 95. Early in the next century Pliny, the governor of Bithynia, writes that he routinely imprisoned and punished any who were found to be Christians, though he himself thought them harmless.

Above
A sign recognized by Christians everywhere.

Before he arrived in Rome Paul made three great journeys through what is now Syria, Turkey and Greece. There he taught the message of Christ and founded Christian communities. Not everything went smoothly, so Paul wrote to them, explaining, correcting, encouraging and praising their efforts. These letters which were read out were mostly addressed to the whole community. Often a letter was passed from one community to another. Paul also wrote to individuals. The Bible has twelve letters attributed to Paul. Some of these may be two or three letters put one after the other without a break. No doubt some letters have been completely lost.

(In the New Testament, these letters are not printed in the order in which they were written, but in order of decreasing length. This can be confusing.)

The letters give a vivid impression of a fiery personality, passionately concerned about his communities, and fiercely protective of them. He obviously liked some communities better than others. Writing to the Galatians, he loses his temper and calls them "senseless fools". He had a special affection for the Christians at Philippi. They were the only community from whom he would accept a gift of money.

Letter-writing was well developed and besides the official imperial postal-system, travellers would carry letters for friends. Letters were addressed and signed at the beginning: *X sends greeting to Y*. Paul always begins his letters with the Christian greeting of "grace and peace".

Letters to Thessalonica

The earliest letters are two to the community at Thessalonica. Paul had taught them that Christ had conquered death and would soon return to take with him all his followers in a sort of heavenly triumphal procession. But some of the community had died; what would happen to them? Paul tells them not to worry about those who "have fallen asleep in Jesus". When Christ returns, "they will be the first to rise, and then the rest of us, who remain alive, will be taken up to meet the Lord in the air". None of this, however, will happen until there has been a difficult period of trials and persecution.

Letters to the Corinthians

One very troublesome community was at Corinth. They were a mixed community, made up of philosophers from the university there and dock-workers from the two ports, some rich, some poor. They were very conscious of the power of Christ's Spirit among them, but they were a deeply divided community, who did not mind upsetting each other. Paul writes to them that the greatest gift of all is love: "If I can speak all languages, human and angelic, but speak without love, I am no more than a gong booming or a cymbal clashing."

Letters to the Philippians

Writing to his friends at Philippi, Paul shows how important to him was Christ's death and resurrection. He quotes a hymn which was already used in the Christian assembly: "Christ was so humble that he even accepted death, death on a cross. And for this God raised him up, so that all beings should bend the knee at the name of Jesus, and acknowledge Jesus Christ as Lord."

Letters to the Galatians and Romans

Two of Paul's letters (to the communities in Galatia and at Rome) show him tussling with the relationship between Christianity and the Jewish religion. He finds it agonizing that so few Jews have become Christians, when for him Jesus is the completion of all the Jewish hopes. He sees the Jewish Law as leading people to Christ, as a slave used to lead children to school. "I am certain of this, neither death nor life, nor angels nor any created thing, will be able to come between us and the love of God made known to us in Jesus Christ." In this way, Paul sees Christ as the fulfilment of the Scriptures, and the key to all life.

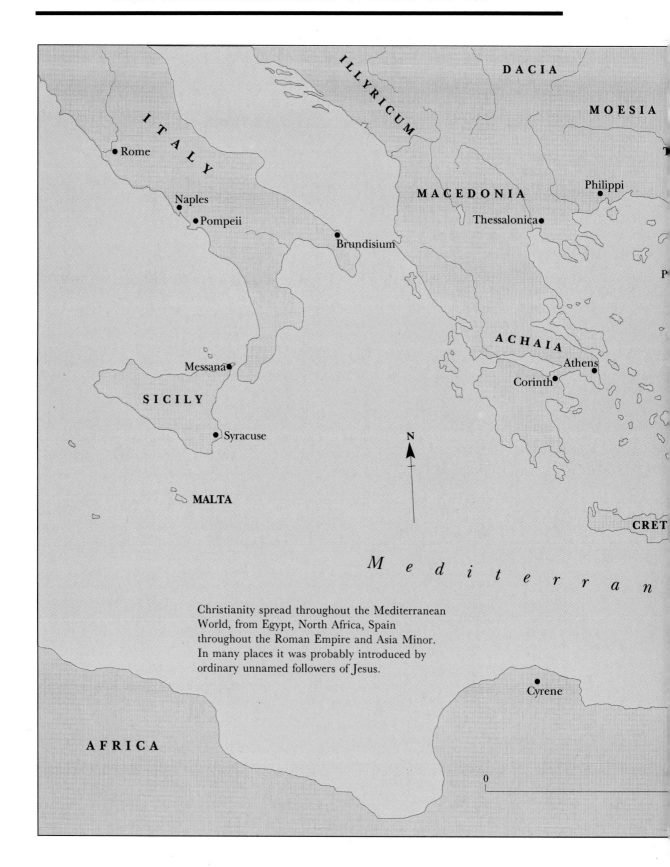

Christianity spread throughout the Mediterranean World, from Egypt, North Africa, Spain throughout the Roman Empire and Asia Minor. In many places it was probably introduced by ordinary unnamed followers of Jesus.

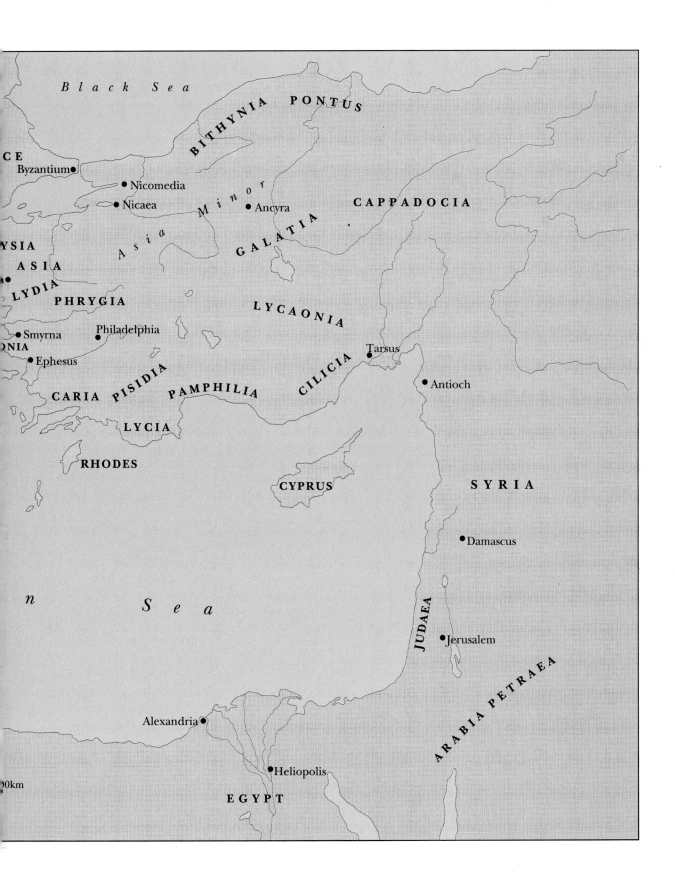

Black Sea

BITHYNIA PONTUS

CE

Byzantium●

●Nicomedia

●Nicaea

Asia Minor

●Ancyra

CAPPADOCIA

GALATIA

YSIA

ASIA

LYDIA

PHRYGIA

LYCAONIA

Smyrna●

●Philadelphia

ONIA

●Ephesus

Tarsus

CARIA

PISIDIA

PAMPHILIA

CILICIA

●Antioch

LYCIA

RHODES

CYPRUS

SYRIA

n

Sea

●Damascus

JUDAEA

●Jerusalem

ARABIA PETRAEA

Alexandria●

)0km

●Heliopolis

EGYPT

245

In our New Testaments the books are not printed in the order in which they were written. The gospels are given pride of place by being printed first although they were written after Paul's letters. After the gospels is Acts.

Next the letters of Paul are printed, but again not in the order in which they were written: they are in two groups: those written to communities and those written to individuals. Within these groups they are printed in order of length, the longest first and the shortest last.

Then come the other letters, and finally the Book of Revelation.

THE LETTERS OF PAUL

Between AD 51 and 62 the apostle Paul wrote a number of letters to the communities he founded round the eastern shores of the Mediterranean. He wrote to encourage them, to answer their questions and to solve problems which were worrying them. These letters were collected together within fifty years.

Early letters (AD 51–52)
1–2 Thessalonians   The Christians at Thessalonica were worried because some of their number had died before the expected coming of Christ.

The Four "Great" letters (AD 55–57)
Galatians   Some Jewish Christians were trying to persuade the community in Galatia (central Turkey) to keep to Jewish customs.

THE FOUR GOSPELS

The stories about Jesus' life and teaching were passed on by word of mouth among his followers for some thirty years before they were written down. Scholars dispute which gospel was written first. Most early Christian writers thought Matthew was the first gospel, but most modern scholars think Mark was earlier.

 MARK

The Gospel according to Mark   This is the shortest of the gospels. It concentrates on the wonderful personality of Jesus, and on his suffering and death, but does not contain so much of his teaching. Mark probably wrote about AD 65. He wrote in very rough Greek, the sort of language slaves would have spoken.

 MATTHEW

The Gospel according to Matthew   This gospel probably used Mark, and other special memories of Matthew. It contains a lot more of Jesus' teaching; this may come from a collection of sayings of Jesus. The gospel is linked to Matthew, the tax-collector of Capernaum; it set out to show that Jesus fulfilled Jewish hopes, so it may have been written especially for Christian converts from Judaism.

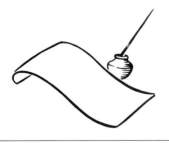

THE GENERAL LETTERS

The remaining letters of the New Testament are not addressed to any particular community, as Paul's letters were. All (except Hebrews) claim to be written by one of the apostles.

The Letter to the Hebrews   A letter written to Christian converts from Judaism, to show that the sacrifice of Jesus is more perfect than the Jewish sacrifices in the Temple.

THE BOOK OF REVELATION

This is a series of visions described by John, and placed at the end of the New Testament. It uses rich symbols from the Old Testament. It was written (perhaps in AD 68, perhaps in AD 90) to encourage persecuted Christians that God would look after them and reward them in the end. It describes vividly the final battle between the forces of good and the forces of evil.

Paul replied that faith in Christ alone was sufficient for salvation.

Romans Paul returns to this great theme when he writes to the large Christian community at Rome to explain how Christianity completes Judaism.

1–2 Corinthians Corinth was a large port, and had a large and varied Christian community. Paul wrote several times to settle differences among them. His explanations of Christian love are especially important.

The letters from Captivity, written when Paul was in prison in Caesarea and Rome (AD 60–62)

Philippians A specially intimate letter to Paul's favorite community at Philippi.

Colossians Paul writes to the Christians at Colossae (in Turkey) to explain that Christ is supreme over all the universe.

Ephesians A letter to Ephesus, very similar to the letter to Colossae. It also stresses that all Christians must be united.

Philemon A short personal letter to a friend, sending back to him a slave who had run away to Paul.

The "Pastoral" letters address pastoral concerns in the Christian community.

1–2 Timothy Letters to Paul's disciple, Timothy.

Titus A similar letter to his disciple, Titus.

LUKE *The Gospel according to Luke** This gospel also probably used Mark, and either the same collection of sayings of Jesus or Matthew's gospel. Luke was possibly a companion of Paul. He wrote for a rather well-to-do audience in the Greek-speaking world. The same author wrote a second volume, the ***Acts of the Apostles**, about how Christianity spread in Palestine, Greece and eventually Rome.

JOHN *The Gospel according to John** This gospel is quite different to the other three. It uses fewer and longer stories about Jesus. There are many symbols: Jesus calls himself the Light of the World, the Good Shepherd, the Resurrection and the Life. The gospel is based on the witness of the beloved disciple, who is perhaps John, one of Jesus' earliest companions.

The Letter of James Some think this the earliest writing of the New Testament, from about AD 50. It gives advice about Christian behavior, especially the rich and the poor.

Three Letters of John The first letter especially concentrates on Christian love, both how Christ loves human beings and how human beings love Christ. The other two are very short.

Two Letters of Peter The first letter is written to guide newly-baptized Christians. The second letter teaches how to deal with evil doers and false teachers who have come into the church.

The Letter of Jude A short letter for Christian converts from Judaism.

* Books referred to in Bible Alive

OLD TESTAMENT Chronology

PALESTINE	THE REST OF THE WORLD
Before Christ	
c3000	Pyramids built in Egypt
	Emergence of city states with kings in Mesopotamia
	Royal graves at Ur
c2000 Potters start to use a wheel in Palestine	
1792	Hammurabi's Laws recorded in Babylon
1720	Hyksos take control of Egypt
1550	Egyptians regain power; expel the Hyksos
c1300	Alphabetic writing first used at Ugarit
c1200	Collapse of the Hittite empire
	Trojan War
	Hill-forts developed in Europe
1000 David captures Jerusalem	Foundation of the Assyrian empire
c965 Solomon assumes the throne in Israel	
931 Division of the Hebrew Kingdom	
c850	First Olympic Games
c750	First Greek colonies around the Mediterranean
722 Israel absorbed by Assyrian empire	
700	Greek city states established
612	Fall of Assyrian empire
597 Nebuchadnezar II exiles Jehoiachin to Babylon	First Greek coins
587 Fall of Jerusalem	Roman Republic established
	Release of Jehoiachin
550	Achaemenid empire of Persia established
c520 Rebuilding of Temple at Jerusalem	
c500	First canal connecting the Nile and the Red Sea completed
c490	Battle of Marathon
	Persians repelled from Europe
445 Nehemiah rebuilds walls of Jerusalem	Athenian empire dominates Greece
334 Alexander the Great invades Asia Minor; he defeats Persia and Egypt	
323 Seleucid Empire established	Death of Alexander
305	Ptolemies control Egypt
250	Rome controls all the Italian peninsular
167 Maccabean revolt against Seleucids	
164 The Temple in Jerusalem is rededicated (Hanukkah)	Rome conquers Greek states
134 Hasmonaean Dynasty established in Judaea	
63 Arrival of Romans in Palestine under Pompey the Great	
44	Assassination of Julius Caesar
37 Herod the Great, King of Judaea	
27	Augustus declared first Roman emperor
19 Rebuilding of the Temple in Jerusalem completed in AD 64	
4 Death of King Herod	

PALESTINE	THE REST OF THE WORLD
Before Christ	
6–4 BC Birth of Jesus of Nazareth	
4 BC Appointment of King Herod's sons over his divided kingdom: Archelaus enthnarch in Judaea Philip tetrarach in Batanaea Herod Antipas tetrarch in Galilee	
Anno Domini	
6 Judaea becomes a Roman province under a prefect. Archelaus dismissed	
6 Tax census of Quirinius	
14	Death of Augustus Tiberius emperor in Rome until AD 37
c30 Beginning of Jesus' public ministry	
c33 Crucifixion of Jesus	
26–36 Pontius Pilate, prefect of Judaea	
c36 Conversion of Paul	
37–39	Pogrom against the Jews of Alexandria. Gaius (Caligula) emperor in Rome until AD 41
41–44 Herod Agrippa I, King of Judaea and Samaria	Claudius emperor in Rome until AD 54
43	Roman invasion of Britain
44 Judaea under direct Roman rule	
45–49 Paul's first missionary journey	Jews expelled from Rome in AD 49
50–52 Paul's second missionary journey	
50	Population in Rome reaches 1 million
53–58 Paul's third missionary journey	
54	Nero emperor in Rome until AD 68
64	First persecution of Christians in Rome
66 First Jewish revolt against Rome in Palestine. Jewish Christians flee to Pella	
70 Destruction of Jerusalem by the Romans	
79	Mount Vesuvius erupts and entombs Pompeii and Herculaneum
88	Persecution of Christians in Rome under the Emperor Domitian

Abraham father of nations

Adam man

Adonai Hebrew for "the Lord" used by the Jews because they considered God's personal name "Yahweh" too sacred to pronounce

angels messengers sent bearing instructions, news, or warnings

anoint a ceremony in which oil is poured on the head to set a person apart for God's work

apostle means "one sent". It is used especially to refer to the first disciples sent out by Jesus

Aramaic a language closely related to Hebrew originally it was the language of trade and diplomacy throughout the area. Eventually it replaced Hebrew as the language used by most people

Ark of the Covenant the sacred box containing the tablets of stone inscribed with the Laws given to Moses

baptism ritual washing with water as a sign of personal purification. Christian baptism is a sign of admission to the community

bride-price a traditional gift from the bridegroom to the bride's family

Canaan the ancient name for the land (more or less the area of modern Israel), inhabited by the Canaanites before Abraham, and gradually conquered by the Israelites under and after Joshua

Christ a Greek word meaning "anointed", title given to Jesus (see also Messiah)

circumcision removal of foreskin covering the penis, a religious practice among the Jews and other Semitic people

covenant a binding agreement. It is God's commitment to the Israelites as his chosen people and their commitment to worship God alone

Day of Atonement: *Yom Kippur* the most solemn fast in the Jewish calendar when animal sacrifice was made to atone for sin

diakonia Greek word meaning "service". The base for our modern English word deacon, one who serves

disciple a personal follower used especially of Jesus' first followers

ekklesia public assembly, used especially of the sacred assembly of God's people

Eloi, Eloi, lama sabachthani? "My God, my God, why have you forsaken me." Jesus' words from the cross

Epiphany the Feast of Jesus' Appearing, celebrated on January 6th

gentile a non Jew

gospel the good news preached by Jesus. It is also used to refer to the first four books of the New Testament, the record of Jesus' message

Hasidim "the pious", a sect devoted to maintaining the purity of Jewish faith and worship

Hebrew descendants of Abraham. Also the language in which most of the Old Testament is written

Hyksos the shepherd kings of Egypt

I am name of God (Yahweh) revealed to Moses, sometimes "I am what I shall be" or "what I reveal myself to be"

ichthus the Greek word for fish whose letters also stand for the initials *Iesous Christos Theou Uios Soter* meaning "Jesus Christ, Son of God, Savior"

idolatry the worship of idols

Israel a term with three distinct meanings:
1. The chosen people of the Scriptures descended from Jacob, who was given the name Israel
2. The northern part of Palestine, which split off from Judah (the southern part) after the death of Solomon, and was conquered by Assyria in 721 BC
3. The modern State of Israel, declared independent in 1948

GLOSSARY

Judaea the region of Palestine, centered around Jerusalem, occupied by the Jews after their return from exile in Babylon

Judah the southern part of Palestine separated from Israel (the northern part) after the death of Solomon and ruled by descendants of King David

judge an active or militant leader in Israel

martyr Greek for "witness", especially those who witnessed to Christ's message by their death

mercy seat a gold plate on top of the Ark where the Israelites came to ask for God's forgiveness

Mesopotamia the land between the rivers (Tigris and Euphrates) almost the same area as modern Iraq

messiah the aramaic word for "anointed", a title given to Jesus the Messiah (see also Christ)

Muslim a believer in Allah according to the revelation through his prophet Muhammad (died AD 632)

nomads are people who wander from place to place. They survive by living off the land until the immediate resources are used up and they move elsewhere

Palestine most of the land previously known as Canaan and renamed after the Philistines who settled in the southern region.

parable stories told by Jesus to illustrate the nature and demands of his coming kingdom

Passover a feast in remembrance of God's deliverance of the Israelites from slavery in Egypt

pharaoh king of Egypt

Pharisee or "separate ones", a sect of the Jews concerned with an exact interpretation of the Law

phylactery a small leather box containing part of the Jewish Law and bound to the head and left hand and arm by some during prayer, also known as tefillin

prophet has two meanings
1. travelling group of professional seers or future tellers
2. those who preached and proclaimed the word of God, speaking directly in the name of God

rabbi Hebrew for "my master", a term used of Jewish teachers

Sabbath the weekly Jewish holy day, Saturday

Sadducees the priestly families of the Temple in Jesus' time

superstition a belief in the power of magic and charms. Often including an unreasonable fear of the mysterious

synoptic gospels are the first three gospels, Matthew, Mark and Luke, which share roughly the same order of events in Jesus' life, from the Greek words meaning "to see together"

Tabernacle the tent in which the Israelites carried the Ark of the Covenant when travelling through the desert, also called the Tent of Meeting, as the place where Israel could come into God's presence

Torah the Jewish religious law, especially the first five books of the Bible

Yahweh the distinctive word for the name of God (see **I am** above). Conventionally translated as "the Lord"

Zion was God's holy hill at Jerusalem, used by the poets and psalmists to mean God's dwelling place

INDEX

INDEX

ACKNOWLEDGEMENTS

BIBLE ALIVE PHOTOGRAPHY

Production Management	**Al Raz Film Services** **Asher Gat, Eitan Alon**
Production Secretaries	**El Glinoer, Sigal Barak** Olivia Slot
Location Manager	**Raz Haen**
Make-up	**Maskit Koren** Michelle Bayliss
Wardrobe	**Shimon Elemelech** Ada Levin, Jack Bitton
Casting	**Zeev Zigler,** Zvia Zilberberg
Props, design, construction	**Gil Ifergan, Daniel Kantor** Itzik Nofar, Irit Wilkansky, Ron Hardie
Processing	**Studio M, Tel Aviv** Metro, London
Film stock	**Fuji**
Travel	**Orientours,** El Al
Locations used by kind permission of	**Israel National Reserves Authority** **Israel National Parks Authority** **Ecole Biblique et Archeologique, Jerusalem** Model City of Jerusalem from the **Holylands Hotel, Jerusalem**
Photographic credits	**Biophotos, Tony Stone Worldwide**
Museums collections reproduced by kind permission of	**Hazor Museum** **Bible Lands Museum, Jerusalem**
Maps created by	**Swanston Graphics, Derby**